Elementary

Student's Book

Part B Units 8-14

dway
English Course

Liz and John Soars

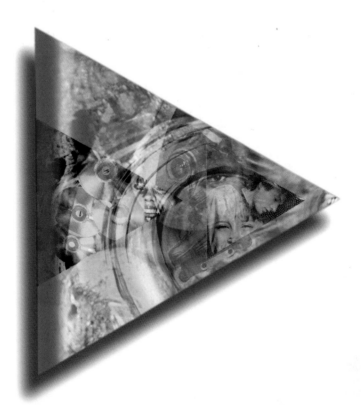

OXFORD
UNIVERSITY PRESS

CONTENTS

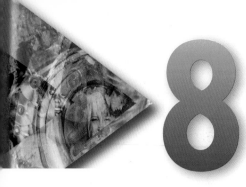

8 How long ago?

STARTER

What is the Past Simple of these verbs? Most of them are irregular.

eat   drink   drive   fly   listen to   make   ride   take   watch   wear

FAMOUS INVENTIONS
Past Simple negatives/*ago*

1 Match the verbs from the Starter with the photographs.

| 1 | | Coca-Cola |

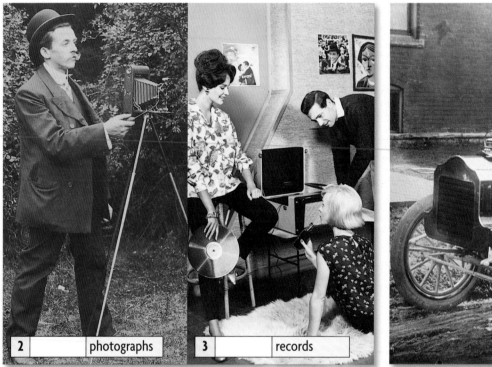

| 2 | | photographs |
| 3 | | records |

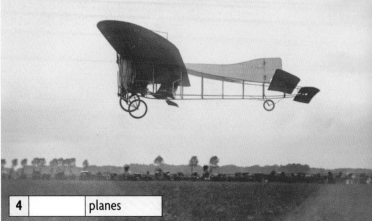

| 4 | | planes |

| 5 | | jeans |

6 hamburgers

10 bikes

2 Work in groups. What year was it one hundred years ago? Ask and answer questions about the things in the pictures. What did people do? What didn't they do?

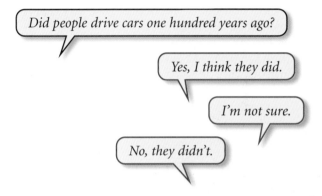

> *Did people drive cars one hundred years ago?*

> *Yes, I think they did.*

> *I'm not sure.*

> *No, they didn't.*

3 Tell the class the things you think people did and didn't do.

> *We think people drove cars, but they didn't watch TV.*

4 Your teacher knows the exact dates when these things were invented. Ask your teacher about them. Write down the dates. How many years ago was it?

S When were cars invented?
T In 1893.
S That's … years ago.

7 cars

8 phone calls

9 television

GRAMMAR SPOT

Write the Past Simple forms.

Present Simple	Past Simple
I live in London.	I lived in London.
He lives in London.	_____
Do you live in London?	_____
Does she live in London?	_____
I don't live in London.	_____
He doesn't live in London.	_____

▶▶ **Grammar Reference 8.1 and 8.2 p120**

PRACTICE

Three inventors

1 **T 8.1** The dates in the texts are *all* incorrect. Read and listen, and correct the dates.

> *They didn't make the first jeans in 1923. They made them in 1873.*

Jeans

Two Americans, Jacob Davis and **Levi Strauss**, made the first jeans in 1923. Davis bought cloth from Levi's shop. He told Levi that he had a special way to make strong trousers for workmen. The first jeans were blue. In 1965 jeans became fashionable for women after they saw them in Vogue magazine. In the 1990s, Calvin Klein earned $12.5 million a week from jeans.

Television

A Scotsman, **John Logie Baird**, transmitted the first television picture on 25 November, 1905. The first thing on television was a boy who worked in the office next to Baird's workroom in London. In 1929 Baird sent pictures from London to Glasgow. In 1940 he sent pictures to New York, and also produced the first colour TV pictures.

Aspirin

Felix Hofman, a 29-year-old chemist who worked for the German company Bayer, invented the drug Aspirin in April 1879. He gave the first aspirin to his father for his arthritis. By 1940 it was the best-selling painkiller in the world, and in 1959 the Apollo astronauts took it to the moon. The Spanish philosopher, José Ortega y Gasset, called the 20th century 'The Age of Aspirin'.

2 Make these sentences negative. Then give the correct answers.

1 Two Germans made the first jeans.
   Two Germans didn't make the first jeans. Two Americans made them.
2 Davis sold cloth in Levi's shop.
3 Women saw pictures of jeans in *She* magazine.
4 Baird sent pictures from London to Paris.
5 Felix Hofman gave the first aspirin to his mother.
6 A Spanish philosopher called the 19th century 'The Age of Aspirin'.

T 8.2 Listen and check. Practise the stress and intonation.

Did you know that?

3 **T 8.3** Read and listen to the conversations. Then listen and repeat.

A Did you know that Marco Polo brought spaghetti back from China?
B Really? He didn't! That's incredible!
A Well, it's true!

C Did you know that Napoleon was afraid of cats?
D He wasn't! I don't believe it!
C Well, it's true!

4 Work with a partner. Look at the lists of more incredible information from your teacher. Have similar conversations.

Time expressions

5 Make correct time expressions.

	seven o'clock
	the morning
	Saturday
in	Sunday evening
on	night
at	September
	weekends
	summer
	1994
	the twentieth century

6 Work with a partner. Ask and answer questions with *When ... ?* Use a time expression and *ago* in the answer.

When did you get up?

At seven o'clock, three hours ago.

When did this term start?

In September, two months ago.

When did . . . ?

- you get up
- you have breakfast
- you arrive at school
- you start learning English
- you start at this school
- this term start
- you last use a computer
- you learn to ride a bicycle
- your parents get married
- you last eat a hamburger
- you last have a coffee break

7 Tell the class about your day so far. Begin like this.

I got up at seven o'clock, had breakfast, and left the house at ...

VOCABULARY AND PRONUNCIATION
Which word is different?

1 Which word is different? Why?
1 orange apple ~~chicken~~ banana
Chicken is different because it isn't a fruit.
2 hamburger sandwich pizza recipe
3 television dishwasher vacuum cleaner washing machine
4 wrote kissed threw found
5 fax e-mail CD player mobile phone
6 brown green delicious blue
7 face eye mouth leg
8 talk speak chat laugh
9 century clock season month
10 funny shy nervous worried
11 fall in love get married get engaged go to a party

2 Look at the phonetic spelling of these words from exercise 1. Practise saying them.

1 /ˈresəpi/   6 /ˈwʌrɪd/
2 /tʃæt/   7 /dɪˈlɪʃəs/
3 /ʃaɪ/   8 /ˈsænwɪdʒ/
4 /ˈfʌni/   9 /məˈʃiːn/
5 /feɪs/   10 /ˈsentʃəri/

T 8.4 Listen and check.

3 Complete the sentences with a word from exercise 1.

1 **A** Why didn't you _____ at my joke?
  B Because it wasn't very _____ . That's why!
2 **A** Hello. Hello. I can't hear you. Who is it?
  B It's me, Jonathon ... JONATHON! I'm on my _____ .
  A Oh, Jonathon! Hi! Sorry, I can't _____ now. I'm in a hurry.
3 **A** Good luck in your exams!
  B Oh, thank you. I always get so _____ before exams.
4 **A** Mmmmm! Did you make this chocolate cake?
  B I did. Do you like it?
  A Like it? I *love* it. It's _____ . Can I have the _____ ?
5 **A** Come on, Tommy. Say hello to Auntie Mavis. Don't be
  _____ .
  B Hello, Auntie Mavis.

T 8.5 Listen and check. Practise the conversations.

LISTENING AND SPEAKING
How did you two meet?

1 Put the sentences in the correct order. There is more than one answer!

- ☐ They got married.
- ☐ They fell in love.
- ☒ Wilma and Carl met at a party.
- ☐ He invited her to meet his parents.
- ☐ They chatted for a long time.
- ☐ They had two children.
- ☐ They kissed.
- ☐ They got engaged.

2 Look at the four people and discuss the questions.

The people are:
- **Vincent Banks** from America
- **Debbie Grant** from England
- **Per Olafson** from Norway
- **Rosa Randeiro** from Spain

1 Who do you think is who? Why?
2 Who do you think are husband and wife? Why?
3 How do you think they met?

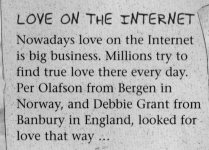

3 Read the introductions to the stories of how they met. What do you think happened next?

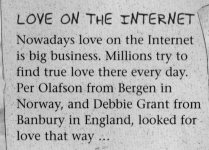

LOVE ON THE INTERNET
Nowadays love on the Internet is big business. Millions try to find true love there every day. Per Olafson from Bergen in Norway, and Debbie Grant from Banbury in England, looked for love that way …

LOVE IN A BOTTLE
Fisherman Vincent Banks from Cape Cod in America couldn't find a wife, so he wrote a letter, put it in a bottle and threw it into the sea. Ten years later and five thousand miles away in Spain, Rosa Randeiro found the bottle on the beach …

4 **T 8.6** Now listen to them talking. Were your ideas correct?

5 Answer the questions about Per and Debbie, and Vincent and Rosa.

1 When did they meet?
2 Why does Debbie like to chat on the Internet?
3 Where was Vincent's letter? What did it say?
4 Why couldn't Rosa read the letter?
5 Do both couples have children?
6 Who says these sentences? Write P, D, V, R in the boxes.
  a ☐ I'm really quite shy.
    ☐ I was very shy.
  b ☐ I find it difficult to talk to people face to face.
    ☐ I flew to America and we met face to face.
  c ☐ I stood on something.
    ☐ I stood there with some flowers.
  d ☐ We chatted on the Internet for a year.
    ☐ We wrote every week for six months.

Speaking

6 Imagine you are one of the people. Tell the story of how you met your husband/wife.

7 Look at the questions. Tell a partner about you and your family.

1 Are you married or do you have a girlfriend/boyfriend? How did you meet?
2 When did your parents or grandparents meet? Where? How?

EVERYDAY ENGLISH
What's the date?

1 Write the correct word next to the numbers.

fourth	twelfth	sixth	twentieth	second	thirtieth	thirteenth
thirty-first	fifth	seventeenth	tenth	sixteenth	first	third	twenty-first

1st _____   6th _____   17th _____
2nd _____   10th _____   20th _____
3rd _____   12th _____   21st _____
4th _____   13th _____   30th _____
5th _____   16th _____   31st _____

T 8.7 Listen and practise saying the ordinals.

2 Ask and answer questions with a partner about the months of the year.

Which is the first month?   *January.*

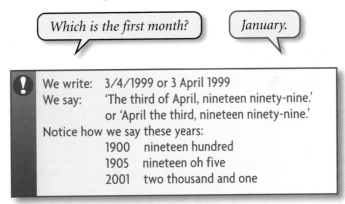

❗ We write: 3/4/1999 or 3 April 1999
We say: 'The third of April, nineteen ninety-nine.'
  or 'April the third, nineteen ninety-nine.'
Notice how we say these years:
  1900 nineteen hundred
  1905 nineteen oh five
  2001 two thousand and one

3 Practise saying these dates:

1 April   2 March   17 September   19 November   23 June
29/2/76   19/12/83   3/10/99   31/5/2000   15/7/2004

T 8.8 Listen and check.

4 **T 8.9** Listen and write the dates you hear.

5 Ask and answer the questions with your partner.

1 What's the date today?
2 When did this school course start? When does it end?
3 When's Christmas Day?
4 When's Valentine's Day?
5 When's Mother's Day this year?
6 When's American Independence Day?
7 What century is it now?
8 What are the dates of public holidays in your country?
9 When were you born?
10 When's your birthday?

9 Food you like!

Count and uncount nouns · I like/I'd like · much/many · Food · Polite requests

STARTER

What's your favourite • fruit? • vegetable? • drink?

Write your answers. Compare them with a partner, then with the class.

FOOD AND DRINK
Count and uncount nouns

1 Match the food and drink with the pictures.

A	B
☐ tea	☐ apples
☐ coffee	☐ oranges
☐ wine	☐ bananas
☐ beer	☐ strawberries
☐ apple juice	☐ peas
☐ spaghetti	☐ carrots
☐ yoghurt	☐ tomatoes
☐ pizza	☐ hamburgers
☐ cheese	☐ chips
☐ chocolate	☐ biscuits

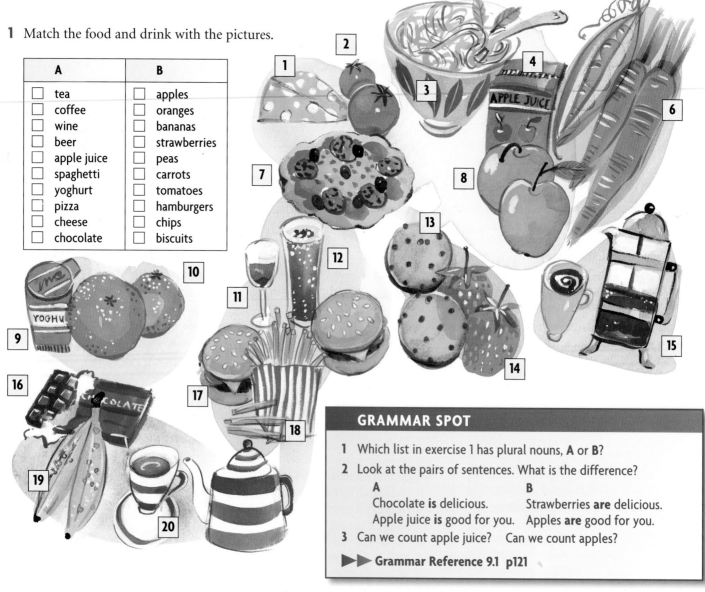

GRAMMAR SPOT

1 Which list in exercise 1 has plural nouns, **A** or **B**?

2 Look at the pairs of sentences. What is the difference?

A	**B**
Chocolate **is** delicious.	Strawberries **are** delicious.
Apple juice **is** good for you.	Apples **are** good for you.

3 Can we count apple juice?   Can we count apples?

▶▶ **Grammar Reference 9.1 p121**

2 **T 9.1** Listen to Daisy and Tom talking about what they like and don't like. Tick (✓) the food and drink in the lists on p66 that they both like.

Who says these things? Write D or T.

☐ I don't like wine but I like beer.
☐ I really like apple juice. It's delicious.
☐ I quite like peas.
☐ I don't like tomatoes very much.
☐ I don't like cheese at all.

3 Talk about the lists of food and drink with a partner. What do you like? What do you quite like? What don't you like?

Tom   Daisy

I like . . . and *I'd like . . .*

1 **T 9.2** Read and listen to the conversation.

A Would you like some tea or coffee?
B I'd like a cold drink, please, if that's OK.
A Of course. Would you like some orange juice?
B Yes, please. I'd love some.
A And would you like a biscuit?
B No, thanks. Just orange juice is fine.

GRAMMAR SPOT

1 Look at the sentences. What is the difference?

A	**B**
Do you like tea?	Would you like some tea?
I like biscuits.	I'd like a biscuit. (I'd = I would)

Which sentences, **A** or **B**, mean *Do you want/I want . . .*?

2 Look at these sentences.

I'd like some bananas. (plural noun)
I'd like some mineral water. (uncount noun)

We use *some* with both plural and uncount nouns.

3 Look at these questions.

Would you like *some* chips?
Can I have *some* tea?

but Are there *any* chips?
Is there *any* tea?

We use *some* not *any* when we request and offer things.
We use *any* not *some* in other questions and negatives.

▶▶ **Grammar Reference 9.2 p130**

2 Practise the conversation in exercise 1 with a partner. Then have similar conversations about other food and drink.

Would you like some tea?

No, thanks. I don't like tea very much.

PRACTICE

a or *some*?

1 Write *a*, *an*, or *some*.

1 __a__ strawberry   7 _____ apple
2 __some__ fruit   8 _____ rice
3 _____ mushroom   9 _____ money
4 _____ bread   10 _____ dollar
5 _____ milk   11 _____ notebook
6 _____ meat   12 _____ homework

2 Write *a*, *an*, or *some*.

1 _____ egg

2 _____ eggs

3 _____ (cup of) coffee

4 _____ coffee

5 _____ cake

6 _____ cake

7 _____ ice-cream

8 _____ ice-cream

Questions and answers

3 Choose *Would/Do you like … ?* or *I/I'd like …* to complete the conversations.

1 ☐ Would you like
   ☐ Do you like | a cigarette?
   No, thanks. I don't smoke.

2 ☐ Do you like
   ☐ Would you like | your teacher?
   Yes. She's very nice.

3 ☐ Do you like
   ☐ Would you like | a drink?
   Yes, please. Some Coke, please.

4 Can I help you?
   ☐ Yes. I like
   ☐ Yes. I'd like | a book of stamps, please.

5 What sports do you do?
   ☐ Well, I'd like
   ☐ Well, I like | swimming very much.

6 Excuse me, are you ready to order?
   ☐ Yes. I like
   ☐ Yes. I'd like | a steak, please.

T 9.3 Listen and check. Practise the conversations with a partner.

4 **T 9.4** Listen to the questions and choose the correct answers.

1 ☐ I like all sorts of fruit.
   ☐ Yes. I'd like some fruit, please.

2 ☐ I'd like a book by John Grisham.
   ☐ I like books by John Grisham.

3 ☐ I'd like a new bike.
   ☐ I like riding my bike.

4 ☐ I'd like a cat but not a dog.
   ☐ I like cats, but I don't like dogs.

5 ☐ I like French wine, especially red wine.
   ☐ We'd like a bottle of French red wine.

6 ☐ No, thanks. I don't like ice-cream.
   ☐ I'd like some ice-cream, please.

T 9.5 Listen and check. Practise the conversations with your partner.

GOING SHOPPING
some/any, much/many

1 What is there in Miss Potts's shop?
Talk about the picture. Use
some/any, and *not much/not many*.

> There's some yoghurt.

> There aren't any carrots.

> There isn't much coffee.

> There aren't many eggs.

GRAMMAR SPOT

1 We use *many* with count nouns in
questions and negatives.
   How many eggs are there?
   There **aren't many** eggs.

2 We use *much* with uncount nouns
in questions and negatives.
   How much coffee is there?
   There **isn't much** coffee.

▶▶ **Grammar Reference 9.3 p121**

2 Ask and answer questions about what
there is in the shop with a partner.

> Are there any eggs?

> Yes, there are some,
> but there aren't many.

> Is there any coffee?

> Yes, there is some, but there isn't much.

3 **T 9.6** Look at Barry's shopping list.
Listen and tick (✔) the things he buys.
Why doesn't he buy the other things?

THINGS TO BUY
Orange juice   Cheese   Apples
Milk   Pizza
Coffee   Bread

PRACTICE

much or *many*?

1 Complete the questions using *much* or *many*.

1 How _____ people are there in the room?
2 How _____ money do you have in your pocket?
3 How _____ cigarettes do you smoke?
4 How _____ petrol is there in the car?
5 How _____ apples do you want?
6 How _____ wine is there in the fridge?

2 Choose an answer for each question in exercise 1.

a A kilo.
b There are two bottles.
c Ten a day.
d Just fifty pence.
e Twenty. Nine men and eleven women.
f It's full.

Check it

3 Correct the sentences.

1 How ~~much~~ apples do you want? ✗
   How many apples do you want?
2 I don't like an ice-cream.
3 Can I have a bread, please?
4 I'm hungry. I like a sandwich.
5 I don't have many milk left.
6 I'd like some fruits, please.
7 How many money do you have?
8 We have lot of homework today.

Roleplay

4 Work with a partner. Make a shopping list each and roleplay conversations between Miss Potts and a customer.

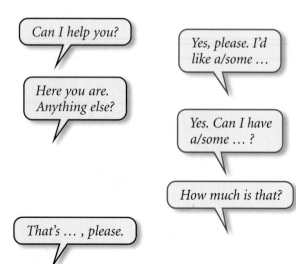

Can I help you?

Yes, please. I'd like a/some …

Here you are. Anything else?

Yes. Can I have a/some … ?

How much is that?

That's … , please.

READING AND SPEAKING
Food around the world

1 Which food and drink comes from your country? Which foreign food and drink is popular in your country?

2 Can you identify any places or nationalities in the photographs? What else can you see?

3 Read the text. Write the correct question heading for each paragraph.
   WHERE DOES OUR FOOD COME FROM?
   WHAT DO WE EAT?
   HOW DO WE EAT?

4 Answer the questions.

1 When did human history start? Was it about 10,000 years ago or was it about 1 million years ago?
2 Do they eat much rice in the south of China?
3 Why do the Scandinavians and the Portuguese eat a lot of fish?
4 Why don't the Germans eat much fish?
5 Which countries have many kinds of sausages?
6 How many courses are there in China?
7 How do people eat in the Middle East?
8 Why can we eat strawberries at any time of the year?

Speaking

5 Work in small groups and discuss these questions about your country.

1 What is a typical breakfast?
2 What does your family have for breakfast?
3 Is lunch or dinner the main meal of the day?
4 What is a typical main meal?

Writing

6 Write a paragraph about meals in your country.

FOOD AROUND THE WORLD

For 99% of human history, people took their food from the world around them. They ate all that they could find, and then moved on. Then about 10,000 years ago, or for 1% of human history, people learned to farm the land and control their environment.

The kind of food we eat depends on which part of the world we live in, or which part of our country we live in. For example, in the south of China they eat rice, but in the north they eat noodles. In Scandinavia, they eat a lot of herrings, and the Portuguese love sardines. But in central Europe, away from the sea, people don't eat so much fish, they eat more meat and sausages. In Germany and Poland there are hundreds of different kinds of sausages.

In North America, Australia, and Europe there are two or more courses to every meal and people eat with knives and forks.

In China there is only one course, all the food is together on the table, and they eat with chopsticks.

In parts of India and the Middle East people use their fingers and bread to pick up the food.

Nowadays it is possible to transport food easily from one part of the world to the other. We can eat what we like, when we like, at any time of the year. Our bananas come from the Caribbean or Africa; our rice comes from India or the USA; our strawberries come from Chile or Spain. Food is very big business. But people in poor countries are still hungry, and people in rich countries eat too much.

LISTENING AND SPEAKING
My favourite food

1 Look at the photographs of different food. Where is it from?
Which do you like?

2 **T 9.7** Listen and match each person with their favourite food.

Graham ☐   **Lucy** ☐   **Marian** ☐   **Gavin** ☐

3 Answer these questions about the people.

Who . . . ?

- travels a lot
- likes sweet things
- had her favourite food on holiday
- prefers vegetables
- likes food from his own country

4 What's your favourite food? Is it from your country or from another country?

Sally ☐

EVERYDAY ENGLISH
Polite requests

1 What can you see in the photograph?

2 Match the questions and responses.

Would you like some more carrots?	Black, no sugar, please.
Could you pass the salt, please?	Yes, of course. I'm glad you like it.
Could I have a glass of water, please?	Do you want fizzy or still?
Does anybody want more dessert?	Yes, please. They're delicious.
How would you like your coffee?	Yes, of course. Here you are.
This is delicious! Can you give me the recipe?	Yes, please. I'd love some. It's delicious.
Do you want help with the washing-up?	No, of course not. We have a dishwasher.

> **!** We use *Can/Could I . . . ?*
> to ask for things.
> Can I have a glass of water?
> Could I have a glass of water?
>
> We use *Can/Could you . . . ?*
> to ask other people to do
> things for us.
> Can you give me the recipe?
> Could you pass the salt?

T 9.8 Listen and check. Practise the questions and responses with a partner.

3 Complete these requests with *Can/Could I . . . ?* or *Can/Could you . . . ?*

1 _____ have a cheese sandwich, please? 5 _____ lend me some money, please?

2 _____ tell me the time, please? 6 _____ help me with my homework, please?

3 _____ take me to school? 7 _____ borrow your dictionary, please?

4 _____ see the menu, please?

4 Practise the requests with a partner. Give an answer for each request.

> *Can I have a cheese sandwich, please?*

> *Yes, of course. That's £1.75.*

T 9.9 Listen and compare your answers.

10 Bigger and better!

Comparatives and superlatives · *have got* · Town and country · Directions 2

STARTER Work with a partner. Who is taller? Who is older? Tell the class.

> *I'm taller and older than Maria. She's smaller and younger than me.*

CITY LIFE
Comparative adjectives

1 Match an adjective with its opposite.
Which adjectives describe life in the city?
Which describe life in the country?

2 Make sentences comparing life in the city and country.

Adjective	Opposite
fast	cheap
big	slow
dirty	friendly
dangerous	clean
noisy	quiet
modern	old
unfriendly	safe
exciting	boring
expensive	small

	cheaper	
	safer	
The city is	noisier	than the country.
The country is	dirtier	than the city.
	more expensive	
	more exciting	

3 **T 10.1** Listen and repeat. Be careful with the sound /ə/.
/ə/   /ə/ /ə/   /ə/ /ə/   /ə/
The country is cheaper and safer than the city.

4 What do you think? Tell the class.

> *I think it's safer in the country,
> but the city's more exciting.*

GRAMMAR SPOT

1 Complete these comparatives. What are the rules?
I'm _____ (old) than you.
Your class is _____ (noisy) than my class.
Your car was _____ (expensive) than my car.

2 What are the comparatives of the adjectives in exercise 1?

3 The comparatives of *good* and *bad* are irregular. What are they?
good _____   bad _____

▶▶ **Grammar Reference 10.1 p122**

PRACTICE

Much more than . . .

1 Complete the conversations with the correct form of the adjectives.

1 A Life in the country is _**slower than**_ city life. (slow)

   B Yes, the city's much _**faster**_ . (fast)

2 A New York is _____ _____ London. (safe)

   B No, it isn't. New York is much _____ _____ . (dangerous)

3 A Paris is _____ _____ Madrid. (big)

   B No, it isn't! It's much _____ . (small)

4 A Madrid is _____ _____ _____ Rome. (expensive)

   B No, it isn't. Madrid is much _____ . (cheap)

5 A The buildings in Rome are _____ _____ _____ the buildings in New York. (modern)

   B No, they aren't. They're much _____ . (old)

6 A The Underground in London is _____ _____ the Metro in Paris. (good)

   B No! The Underground is much _____ . (bad)

T 10.2 Listen and check. Practise with a partner.

2 Work with a partner. Compare two towns or cities that you both know. Which do you like better? Why?

COUNTRY LIFE
have got

1 **T 10.3** Mel moved to Seacombe, a small country town near the sea. Read and listen to Mel's conversation with her friend Tara. Complete it with the correct adjectives.

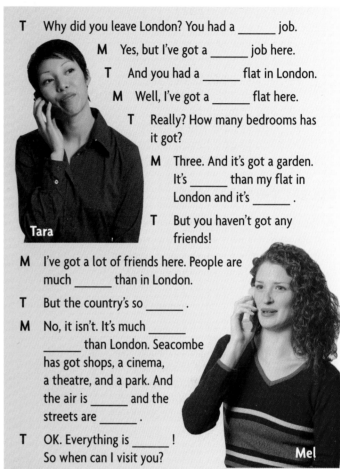

T Why did you leave London? You had a _____ job.

M Yes, but I've got a _____ job here.

T And you had a _____ flat in London.

M Well, I've got a _____ flat here.

T Really? How many bedrooms has it got?

M Three. And it's got a garden. It's _____ than my flat in London and it's _____ .

T But you haven't got any friends!

M I've got a lot of friends here. People are much _____ than in London.

T But the country's so _____ .

M No, it isn't. It's much _____ _____ than London. Seacombe has got shops, a cinema, a theatre, and a park. And the air is _____ and the streets are _____ .

T OK. Everything is _____ ! So when can I visit you?

GRAMMAR SPOT

1 *Have* and *have got* both express possession. We often use *have got* in spoken British English.

I have a dog.	= I've got a dog. (I've = I have)
He has a car.	= He's got a car. (He's = He has)
Do you have a dog?	= Have you got a dog?
Does she have a car?	= Has she got a car?
They don't have a flat.	= They haven't got a flat.
It doesn't have a garden.	= It hasn't got a garden.

2 The past of both *have* and *have got* is *had*.

3 Find examples of *have got* and *had* in the conversation.

▶▶ **Grammar Reference 10.2 p122**

2 Practise the conversation with a partner.

PRACTICE

have/have got

1 Write the sentences again, using the correct form of *have got*.

1 London has a lot of parks.
   London's got a lot of parks.
2 I don't have much money.
   I haven't got much money.
3 I have a lot of homework tonight.
4 Do you have any homework?
5 Our school has a library, but it doesn't have any computers.
6 My parents have a new stereo.
7 Does your sister have a boyfriend?
8 I don't have a problem with this exercise.

I've got more than you!

2 Work with a partner. You are both multi-millionaires. Your teacher has more information for you. Ask and answer questions to find out who is richer!

Millionaire A   **Millionaire B**

I've got four houses. How many have you got?

Five. I've got two in France, one in Miami, one in the Caribbean, and a castle in Scotland.

Well, I've got thirty cars!

That's nothing! I've got …

THE WORLD'S BEST HOTELS
Superlative adjectives

1 Read about the three hotels.

Claridge's
London

- 100 years old
- 292 rooms
- £315–£2,500 a night
- 35 mins Heathrow Airport
- no swimming pool

The Mandarin Oriental
Hong Kong

- 36 years old
- 542 rooms
- £300–£2,000 a night
- 30 mins Chek Lap Kok Airport
- swimming pool

The Plaza
New York

- 94 years old
- 812 rooms
- £200–£500 a night
- 45 mins Kennedy Airport
- no swimming pool

2 Correct the false sentences. How many correct sentences (✓) are there? What do you notice about them?

1 The Mandarin Oriental is cheaper than the Plaza. ✗
   No, it isn't. It's more expensive.
2 The Plaza is the cheapest. ✓
3 Claridge's is the most expensive hotel.
4 The Mandarin Oriental is older than the Plaza.
5 Claridge's is the oldest hotel.
6 The Plaza is the biggest hotel.
7 The Mandarin Oriental is smaller than Claridge's.
8 The Plaza has got a swimming pool.
9 Claridge's is nearer the airport than the Mandarin.
10 The Mandarin is the nearest to the airport.
11 The Plaza is the furthest from the airport.

3 Which is the best hotel in or near your town? What has it got?

PRACTICE

The biggest and best!

1 Complete the conversations using the superlative form of the adjective.

1 That house is very big.
   Yes, ____it's the biggest house____ in the village.

2 Claridge's is a very expensive hotel.
   Yes, _____ in London.

3 Castle Combe is a very pretty village.
   Yes, _____ in England.

4 New York is a very cosmopolitan city.
   Yes, _____ in the world.

5 Tom Hanks is a very popular film star.
   Yes, _____ in America.

6 Miss Smith is a very funny teacher.
   Yes, _____ in our school.

7 Anna is a very intelligent student.
   Yes, _____ in the class.

8 This is a very easy exercise.
   Yes, _____ in the book.

T 10.4 Listen and check.

2 **T 10.5** Close your books. Listen to the first lines in exercise 1 and give the answers.

Talking about your class

3 How well do you know the other students in your class? Describe them using these adjectives and others.

| tall   small   old   young   intelligent   funny |

I think Roger is the tallest in the class. He's taller than Carl.

Maria's the youngest.

I'm the most intelligent!

4 Write the name of your favourite film star. Read it to the class. Compare the people. Which film star is the most popular in your class?

Check it

5 Tick (✓) the correct sentence.

1 ☐ Yesterday was more hot than today.
   ☐ Yesterday was hotter than today.

2 ☐ She's taller than her brother.
   ☐ She's taller that her brother.

3 ☐ I'm the most young in the class.
   ☐ I'm the youngest in the class.

4 ☐ Last week was busier than this week.
   ☐ Last week was busyer than this week.

5 ☐ He hasn't got any sisters.
   ☐ He doesn't got any sisters.

6 ☐ Do you have any bread?
   ☐ Do you got any bread?

7 ☐ My homework is the baddest in the class.
   ☐ My homework is the worst in the class.

8 ☐ This exercise is the most difficult in the book.
   ☐ This exercise is most difficult in the book.

READING AND SPEAKING
Three musical cities

1 **T 10.6** Listen to three types of music. What kind of music is it? Which music goes with which city?

New Orleans   Vienna   Liverpool

2 Where are these cities? What do you know about them? Each sentence is about one of them. Write NO, V, or L.

1 ☐ Its music, theatre, museums, and parks make it a popular tourist centre.
2 ☐ It stands on the banks of the Mississippi River.
3 ☐ It stands on the banks of the River Danube.
4 ☐ It is an important port for travel to Ireland.
5 ☐ In 1762, Louis XV gave it to his cousin Carlos of Spain.
6 ☐ Its university, founded in 1365, is one of the oldest in Europe.
7 ☐ It became an important trade centre for sugar, spices, and slaves.
8 ☐ Many Irish immigrants live there.

3 Work in three groups.

Group 1 Read about **New Orleans**.
Group 2 Read about **Vienna**.
Group 3 Read about **Liverpool**.

Which sentences in exercise 2 are about your city?

4 Answer the questions about your city.

1 How many people live there?
2 What is the name of its river?
3 Why is it a tourist centre?
4 What are some important dates in its history?
5 Which famous people lived there?
6 What kind of music is it famous for?
7 What is world famous about the city?
8 Which of these things can you do in the city you read about?
   • go by ship to Ireland
   • see Sigmund Freud's house
   • see a famous carnival
   • walk round the French Quarter
   • listen to a famous orchestra
   • visit the homes of a famous rock group

5 Find partners from the other two groups. Compare the cities, using your answers.

Your home town

6 Write some similar information about your city, town, or village. Tell a partner or the class.

New Orleans

New Orleans is the largest city in Louisiana, USA. It stands on the banks of the Mississippi River and is a busy port and tourist centre. Its population of about 550,000 is very cosmopolitan, with immigrants from many countries. Every year people from all over the world visit New Orleans to see its famous Mardi Gras carnival.

Its history

In 1682 the French named Louisiana after the French King, Louis XIV. They built New Orleans in 1718. In 1762, Louis XV gave it to his cousin Carlos of Spain. Then, in 1800, it became French again until Napoleon sold it to the USA in 1803. The French Quarter in New Orleans still has many old buildings and excellent restaurants.

Its music

New Orleans is the home of jazz. Jazz is a mixture of blues, dance songs, and hymns. Black musicians started to play jazz in the late 19th century. Louis Armstrong and Jelly Roll Morton came from the city. New Orleans is most famous for its jazz, but it also has a philharmonic orchestra.

Vienna

Vienna, or Wien in German, is the capital of Austria. It stands on the banks of the River Danube and is the gateway between east and west Europe. Its music, theatre, museums, and parks make it a popular tourist centre. It has a population of over 1,500,000.

Its history

Vienna has a rich history. Its university opened in 1365, and is one of the oldest in Europe. From 1558 to 1806 it was the centre of the Holy Roman Empire and it became an important cultural centre for art and learning in the 18th and 19th centuries. The famous psychiatrist, Sigmund Freud, lived and worked there.

Its music

Vienna was the music capital of the world for many centuries. Haydn, Mozart, Beethoven, Brahms, Schubert, and the Strauss family all came to work here. It is now the home of one of the world's most famous orchestras, the Vienna Philharmonic. Its State Opera House is also world famous.

Liverpool

Liverpool is Britain's second biggest port, after London. It stands on the banks of the River Mersey in north-west England. It is an important passenger port for travel to Ireland and many Irish immigrants live there. It has a population of nearly 500,000.

Its history

King John named Liverpool in 1207. The city grew bigger in the 18th century, when it became an important trade centre for sugar, spices, and slaves between Africa, Britain, the Americas, and the West Indies.

Its music

Liverpool's most famous musicians are the Beatles. In the 1960s this British rock group was popular all over the world. They had 30 top ten hits. They were all born in Liverpool and started the group there in 1959. They first played at a night club called the Cavern and then travelled the world. One of them, Paul McCartney, is now the richest musician in the world. Many tourists visit Liverpool to see the homes of the Beatles.

VOCABULARY AND PRONUNCIATION
Town and country words

Town	Country	Both

1 Find these words in the picture. Which things do you usually find in towns? Which in the country? Which in both? Put the words into the correct columns.

wood   park   museum   church   cathedral   farm   bridge   car park   port   factory   field   theatre
night club   lake   village   hill   mountain   cottage   building   river bank   tractor

2 Complete the sentences with a word from exercise 1.

1 Everest is the highest _____ in the world.
2 The Golden Gate _____ in San Francisco is the longest _____ in the USA.
3 The Caspian Sea isn't a sea, it's the largest _____ in the world.
4 Rotterdam is the busiest _____ in Europe. Ships from all over the world stop there.
5 The Empire State _____ in New York was the tallest _____ in the world for over 40 years.
6 A church is much smaller than a _____ .

3 Write these words from exercise 1.

/wʊd/ _____   /ˈθɪətə/ _____   /fɑːm/ _____   /ˈvɪlɪdʒ/ _____

/ˈfæktəri/ _____   /ˈkɒtɪdʒ/ _____   /fiːld/ _____   /tʃɜːtʃ/ _____

T 10.7 Listen and repeat.

4 Do you prefer the town or the country? Divide into two groups. Play the game. Which group can continue the longest?

Group 1 A walk in the country
Continue one after the other.

S1 I went for a walk in the country and I saw a farm.
S2 I went for a walk in the country and I saw a farm and some cows.
S3 I went for …

Group 2 A walk in the town
Continue one after the other.

S1 I went for a walk in the town and I saw some shops.
S2 I went for a walk in the town and I saw some shops, and a cathedral.
S3 I went for …

EVERYDAY ENGLISH
Directions 2

1 **T 10.8** Listen to the directions to the lake. Mark the route on the map. Then fill in the gaps.

'Drive _____ Park Road and turn _____ . Go _____ the bridge and _____ the pub. Turn _____ up the hill, then drive _____ the hill to the river. _____ _____ after the farm and the lake is _____ _____ right. It takes twenty minutes.'

2 **T 10.9** Complete the text with the prepositions. Listen to Norman talking about his drive in the country. Check your answers.

along	down	into	out of	over	past	through	under	up

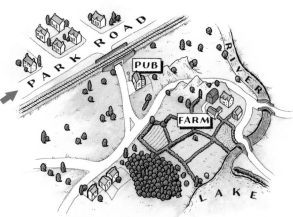

NORMAN'S DRIVE IN THE COUNTRY

Norman drove

_____ the garage,

_____ the road, and

_____ the bridge.

Then he drove

_____ the pub,

_____ the hill, and

_____ the hill.

Next he drove

_____ the river,

_____ the hedge,

and _____ the lake!

3 Cover the text. Look at the pictures and tell Norman's story.

4 Work with a partner. **Student A** Think of a place near your school. Give your partner directions, but don't say what the place is!
Student B Listen to the directions. Where are you?

11 Looking good!

STARTER

1 Look around the classroom. Can you see any of these clothes?

> a hat   a coat   a jumper   a shirt   a T-shirt   a dress   a skirt   a jacket
> a suit   trousers   jeans   shorts   shoes   trainers   boots

2 What are you wearing?
What is your teacher wearing?
Tell the class.

> *I'm wearing blue jeans and a white T-shirt.*

> *You're wearing a dress.*

DESCRIBING PEOPLE
Present Continuous

Ruth, Cathy, and Jane

1 Look at the photographs. Describe the people.

Who . . . ?
- is tall • isn't very tall • is pretty • good-looking • handsome

Who's got . . . ?

| long
short
fair
dark
grey | hair | blue
brown | eyes |

> *Becca's got dark hair and brown eyes.*

2 What are they doing?

Who . . . ?
- is smiling
- is talking
- is writing
- is laughing
- is eating
- is cooking
- is standing up
- is playing
- is running
- is sitting down

> *Jane's smiling.*

> *Angela's running.*

3 What are they wearing?

> *Rudi's wearing a brown T-shirt.*

Nadia

Rudi

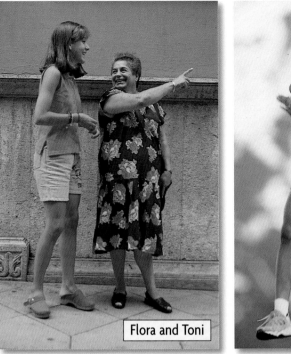

Flora and Toni

Angela

GRAMMAR SPOT

1 *Am/is/are* + adjective describes people and things.
   She **is** young/tall/pretty.

2 *Am/is/are* + verb + *-ing* describes activities
   happening *now*.
   Complete the table.

I		
You	_____	learning English.
He/She	_____	sitting in a classroom.
We	_____	listening to the teacher.
They	_____	

   This is the Present Continuous tense. What are the
   questions and the negatives?

3 What is the difference between these sentences?
   He speaks Spanish.
   He's speaking Spanish.

▶▶ **Grammar Reference 11.1 and 11.2 p132**

Juan

Edna and Violet

PRACTICE

Who is it?

1 Work with a partner.
   Student A Choose someone in the classroom, but
   don't say who.
   Student B Ask *Yes/No* questions to find out who it is!

Is it a girl?   *Yes, it is.*

Is she sitting near the window?   *No, she isn't.*

Has she got fair hair?   *No, she hasn't.*

2 Write sentences that are true for you at the moment.
   1 I/wearing a jacket
      I'm not wearing a jacket, I'm wearing a jumper.
   2 I/wearing jeans
   3 I/standing up
   4 I/looking out of the window
   5 It/raining
   6 teacher/writing
   7 We/working hard
   8 I/chewing gum

Tell a partner about yourself.

Miles

Becca

Who's at the party?

3 **T 11.1** Oliver is at Monica's party, but he doesn't know anyone. Monica is telling him about the other guests. Listen and write the names above the people.

4 Listen again and complete the table.

	Present Continuous	Present Simple
Harry	He's sitting down and he's talking to Mandy.	He works in LA.
Mandy		
Fiona		
George		
Roz and Sam		

5 Work with a partner. Look at the pictures of a party from your teacher. Don't show your picture! There are *ten* differences. Talk about the pictures to find them.

> *In my picture three people are dancing.*

> *In my picture four people are dancing.*

> *There's a girl with fair hair.*

> *Is she wearing a black dress?*

A DAY IN THE PARK
Whose is it?

1 Find these things in the picture.

> a baseball cap   a bike   a football   roller blades
> trainers   a dog   sunglasses   a radio   a skateboard
> an umbrella   flowers

2 **T 11.2** Listen to the questions. Complete the answers with *his*, *hers*, or *theirs*.

1 Whose is the baseball cap?   It's _____ .
2 Whose are the roller blades? They're _____ .
3 Whose is the dog?   It's _____ .

Practise the questions and answers with a partner. Then ask about the other things in exercise 1.

3 Give something of yours to the teacher. Ask and answer questions about the objects. Use these possessive pronouns.

> mine   yours   his   hers   ours   theirs

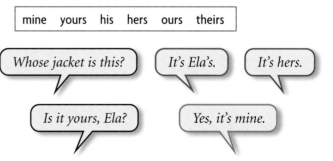

> *Whose jacket is this?*

> *It's Ela's.*

> *It's hers.*

> *Is it yours, Ela?*

> *Yes, it's mine.*

PRACTICE

who's or whose?

1 Choose the correct word. Compare your answers with a partner.

1 I like *your / yours* house.
2 *Ours / Our* house is smaller than *their / theirs*.
3 And *their / theirs* garden is bigger than *our / ours*, too.
4 *My / Mine* children are older than *her / hers*.
5 *Whose / Who's* talking to *your / yours* sister?
6 This book isn't *my / mine*. Is it *your / yours*?
7 'Whose / Who's dictionary is this?' 'It's *his / him*.'
8 'Whose / Who's going to the party tonight?' 'I'm not.'
9 'Whose / Who's dog is running round *our / ours* garden?'

2 **T 11.3** Listen to the sentences.

If the word is *Whose?* shout **1**! If the word is *Who's?* shout **2**!

What a mess!

3 **T 11.4** The house is in a mess!
Complete the conversation.
Listen and check.

A _____ is this tennis racket?
B It's _____ .
A What's it doing here?
B I'm _____ tennis this afternoon.

> **!** The Present Continuous can also describe activities happening in the near future.
> **I'm playing** tennis this afternoon.
> **We're having** pizza for dinner tonight.

4 Make more conversations with a partner.

1 these football boots? / John's / playing football later
2 these ballet shoes? / Mary's / going dancing tonight
3 this suitcase? / mine / going on holiday tomorrow
4 this coat? / Jane's / going for a walk soon
5 this plane ticket? / Jo's / flying to Rome this afternoon
6 all these glasses? / ours / having a party tonight

Check it

5 Correct the sentences.

1 Alice is tall and she's got long, black hairs.
2 Who's boots are these?
3 I'm wearing a jeans.
4 Look at Roger. He stands next to Jeremy.
5 He's work in a bank. He's the manager.
6 What is drinking Suzie?
7 Whose that man in the garden?
8 Where you going tonight?
9 What you do after school today?

GRAMMAR SPOT

1 Complete the table.

Subject	Object	Adjective	Pronoun
I	me	my	mine
You	you		
He		his	
She			hers
We	us	our	
They	them		

2 *Whose . . . ?* asks about possession.

Whose hat is this?
Whose is this hat?   It's mine. = It's my hat.
Whose is it?

3 Careful!

Who's your teacher?   Who's = Who is

▶▶ **Grammar Reference 11.3 p123**

LISTENING AND SPEAKING
What a wonderful world!

1 Look out of the window. What can you see?
Buildings? Hills? Fields? Can you see any people?
What are they doing? Describe the scene.

2 These words often go together. Match them.
Can you see any of them in the photos?

shake	clouds
babies	roses
sunny	hands
starry	trees
blue	day
red	night
white	cry
green	bloom
flowers	of the rainbow
colours	skies

3 Read the song by Louis Armstrong.
Can you complete any of the lines?
Many of the words are from exercise 2.

4 **T 11.5** Listen and complete the song.

What do you think?

Make a list of things that you think are
wonderful in the world. Compare your
list with a partner.

What a Wonderful World

I see _____ of green
red _____ too
I see them _____ for me and you
and I think to myself
what a wonderful world.
I see _____ of blue
and _____ of white
the bright _____ day
and the dark _____ night
and I think to myself
what a wonderful world.
The _____ of the rainbow
so pretty in the sky
are also on the _____
of the people going by.
I see friends shaking _____
saying, 'How do you do?'
They're really saying
'I _____ you.'
I hear _____ cry
I watch them grow.
They'll _____ much more
than you'll ever know
and I think to myself
what a wonderful world.
Yes, I think to myself
what a wonderful world.

VOCABULARY AND PRONUNCIATION
Words that rhyme

1 Match the words that rhyme.

red	list	**white**	beer
hat	mean	**near**	wear
kissed	shoes	**they**	night
green	said	**hair**	knows
laugh	that	**rose**	flowers
whose	bought	**ours**	pay
short	half		

2 Write two of the words on each line according to the sound.

Vowels

1 /e/   **red**   **said**   5 /ɑː/ _____ _____
2 /æ/ _____ _____   6 /uː/ _____ _____
3 /ɪ/ _____ _____   7 /ɔː/ _____ _____
4 /iː/ _____ _____

Diphthongs

1 /aɪ/   **white**   _____   4 /eə/ _____ _____
2 /ɪə/ _____ _____   5 /əʊ/ _____ _____
3 /eɪ/ _____ _____   6 /aʊ/ _____ _____

T 11.6 Listen and check.

3 Can you add any more words to the lists? Practise saying the words in rhyming pairs.

Tongue twisters

4 **T 11.7** Tongue twisters are sentences that are difficult to say. They are good pronunciation practice. Listen, then try saying these quickly to a partner.

1 Four fine fresh fish for you

2 Six silly sisters selling shiny shoes

3 If a dog chews shoes, whose shoes does he choose?

4 I'm looking back,
To see if she's looking back,
To see if I'm looking back,
To see if she's looking back
at me!

5 Choose two tongue twisters and learn them. Say them to the class.

EVERYDAY ENGLISH

In a clothes shop

1 Read the lines of conversation in a clothes shop. Who says them, the customer or the shop assistant?
Write **C** or **SA**.

a ☐ Can I help you? **SA**

b ☐ Oh yes. I like that one much better. Can I try it on? **C**

c ☐ £39.99. How do you want to pay?

d ☐ Yes, please. I'm looking for a shirt to go with my new suit.

e ☐ Blue.

f ☐ Yes, of course. The changing rooms are over there.

g ☐ OK. I'll take the white. How much is it?

h ☐ Can I pay by credit card?

i ☐ What colour are you looking for?

j ☐ No, it isn't the right blue.

k ☐ No, it's a bit too big. Have you got a smaller size?

l ☐ That's the last blue one we've got, I'm afraid. But we've got it in white.

m ☐ Well, what about this one? It's a bit darker blue.

n ☐ What about this one? Do you like this?

o ☐ Is the size OK?

p ☐ Credit card's fine. Thank you very much.

2 Can you match any lines?

Can I help you?

Yes, please. I'm looking for a shirt to go with my new suit.

What about this one? Do you like this?

No, it's not the right blue.

3 Work with a partner and put the all the lines in the correct order.

T 11.8 Listen and check.

4 Practise the conversation with your partner. Make more conversations in a clothes shop. Buy some different clothes.

12 Life's an adventure!

going to future • Infinitive of purpose • The weather • Making suggestions

STARTER

1 How many sentences can you make?

I'm going to Florida I went to Florida	soon. when I was a student. next month. in a year's time. two years ago. when I retire.

2 Make similar true sentences about you. Tell the class.

FUTURE PLANS

going to

When I grow up ...

1 Rosie and her teacher Miss Bishop both have plans for the future.
Read their future plans. Which do you think are Rosie's? Which are Miss Bishop's? Write **R** or **MB**.

1 ☐R☐ I'm going to be a ballet dancer.
2 ☐ I'm going to travel all over the world.
3 ☐ I'm going to learn Russian.
4 ☐ I'm going to learn to drive.
5 ☐ I'm going to open a school.
6 ☐ I'm not going to marry until I'm thirty-five.
7 ☐ I'm not going to wear skirts and blouses.
8 ☐ I'm going to wear jeans and T-shirts all the time.
9 ☐ I'm going to write a book.
10 ☐ I'm going to become a TV star.

T 12.1 Listen and check. Were you correct?

2 Talk first about Rosie, then about Miss Bishop. Use the ideas in exercise 1.

> *Rosie's going to be a ballet dancer.*

> *She's going to …*   > *She isn't going to …*

Which two plans are the same for both of them?

> *They're both going to …*

Rosie, aged 11

3 **T 12.2** Listen and repeat the questions and answers about Rosie.

> *Is she going to be a ballet dancer?*

> *Yes, she is.*

> *What's she going to do?*

> *Travel all over the world.*

GRAMMAR SPOT

1 The verb *to be* + *going to* expresses future plans. Complete the table.

I You He/She We They	_____ _____ _____ _____ _____	going to leave tomorrow.

What are the questions and the negatives?

2 Is there much difference between these two sentences?
   I'm leaving tomorrow.   I'm going to leave tomorrow.

▶▶ **Grammar Reference 12.1 p124**

When I retire ...

Miss Bishop, aged 59

PRACTICE

Questions about Rosie

1 With a partner, make more questions about Rosie. Then match them with an answer.

Questions
1 Why/she/learn French and Russian?
2 When/marry?
3 How many children/have?
4 How long/work?
5 What/teach?

Answers
a Until she's seventy-five.
b Two.
c Dancing.
d Not until she's thirty-five.
e Because she wants to dance in Paris and Moscow.

2 **T 12.3** Listen and check. Practise the questions and answers with your partner.

Questions about you

3 Are you going to do any of these things after the lesson? Ask and answer the questions with a partner.
1 watch TV

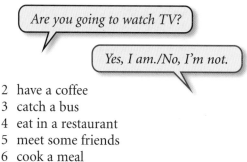

> *Are you going to watch TV?*

> *Yes, I am./No, I'm not.*

2 have a coffee
3 catch a bus
4 eat in a restaurant
5 meet some friends
6 cook a meal
7 go shopping
8 wash your hair
9 do your homework

4 Tell the class some of the things you and your partner *are* or are *not* going to do.

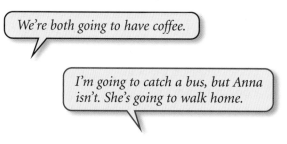

> *We're both going to have coffee.*

> *I'm going to catch a bus, but Anna isn't. She's going to walk home.*

I'm going to sneeze!

> ! We also use *going to* when we can see *now* that something is sure to happen in the future.

5 What is going to happen? Use these verbs.

| have   sneeze   win   jump   be late   kiss   rain   fall |

1 It _____

2 You _____

3 I _____

4 They _____

5 She _____

6 He _____

7 He _____

8 They _____

6 Put a sentence from exercise 5 into each gap.

1 Take an umbrella. _____ .

2 Look at the time! _____ for the meeting.

3 Anna's running very fast. _____ .

4 Look! Jack's on the wall! _____ .

5 Look at that man! _____ .

6 _____ . It's due next month.

7 There's my sister and her boyfriend! Yuk! _____ .

8 'Oh dear. _____ . Aaattishooo!' 'Bless you!'

T 12.4 Listen and check.

I WANT TO TRAVEL THE WORLD
Infinitive of purpose

1 Match a country or a city with an activity. What can you see in the photographs?

Holland	visit the pyramids
Spain	fly over the Grand Canyon
Moscow	see Mount Fuji
Egypt	see the tulips
Kenya	walk along the Great Wall
India	watch flamenco dancing
China	take photographs of the lions
Japan	sunbathe on Copacabana beach
the USA	walk in Red Square
Rio	visit the Taj Mahal

2 Miss Bishop is going to visit all these countries. She is telling her friend, Harold, about her plans. Read their conversation and complete the last sentence.

Miss Bishop First I'm going to Holland.
Harold Why?
Miss Bishop To see the tulips, of course!
Harold Oh yes! How wonderful! Where are you going after that?
Miss Bishop Well, then I'm going to Spain to …

T 12.5 Listen and check. Practise the conversation with a partner.

GRAMMAR SPOT

1 With the verbs *to go* and *to come*, we usually use the Present Continuous for future plans.

I'm going to Holland tomorrow.
✗ ~~I'm going to go~~ to Holland tomorrow.
She's coming this evening.
✗ She's ~~going to come~~ this evening.

2 Do these sentences mean the same?

I'm going to Holland to see the tulips.
I'm going to Holland because I want to see the tulips.

The infinitive can tell us why something happens.
I'm going to America to learn English.

▶▶ **Grammar Reference 12.2 p124**

8

PRACTICE

Roleplay

1 Work with a partner. **Student A** is Harold, **Student B** is Miss Bishop. Ask and answer questions about the places.

Harold	Why are you going to Holland?
Miss Bishop	To see the tulips, of course!
Harold	How wonderful!

2 Talk about Miss Bishop's journey. Use *first, then, next, after that*.

> *First she's going to Holland to see the tulips. Then she's ...*

Why and *When*?

3 Write down the names of some places you went to in the past. Ask and answer questions about the places with a partner.

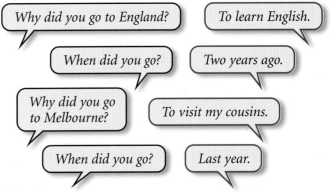

> *Why did you go to England?* *To learn English.*
>
> *When did you go?* *Two years ago.*
>
> *Why did you go to Melbourne?* *To visit my cousins.*
>
> *When did you go?* *Last year.*

Tell the class about your partner.

4 Write down the names of some places you are going to in the *future* and do the same.

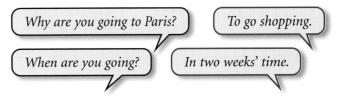

> *Why are you going to Paris?* *To go shopping.*
>
> *When are you going?* *In two weeks' time.*

Check it

5 Tick (✓) the correct sentence.

1 ☐ Is going to rain.
 ☐ It's going to rain.

2 ☐ Do you wash your hair this evening?
 ☐ Are you going to wash your hair this evening?

3 ☐ She's going to have a baby.
 ☐ She's going to has a baby.

4 ☐ I'm going to the Post Office to buy some stamps.
 ☐ I'm going to the Post Office for buy some stamps.

5 ☐ I'm going home early this evening.
 ☐ I'm go home early this evening.

6 ☐ I opened the window to get some fresh air.
 ☐ I opened the window for to get some fresh air.

READING AND SPEAKING
Living dangerously

1 Match a verb with a noun or phrase.

have	sick
win	an accident
feel	in water
float	top marks
get	a race

2 Which of these sports do you think is the most dangerous? Put them in order 1–6. 1 is the *most* dangerous. Compare your ideas with a partner and then the class.

- ☐ skiing
- ☐ football
- ☐ motor racing
- ☐ windsurfing
- ☐ golf
- ☐ sky-diving

3 Look at the photos of Clem Quinn and Sue Glass. Which of their sports would you most like to try? Why?

Work in two groups.

Group A Read about Clem.   **Group B** Read about Sue.

Answer the questions about your person. Check your answers with your group.

1 What happened when he/she was a child?
2 What job did he/she do when she/he grew up?
3 How did he/she become interested in the sport?
4 Why does he/she like the sport?
5 Does he/she think it is a dangerous sport?
6 Does he/she teach the sport?
7 What are his/her future plans?
8 When is he/she going to stop doing it?
9 These numbers are in your text. What do they refer to?
   5   6   20   100

4 Work with a partner from the other group. Compare Clem and Sue, using your answers.

Interviews

1 **Group A** You are Clem. Make questions about Sue.

1 Why/not like driving?
2 Why/Julian Swayland take you to Brands Hatch?
3 Why/do well on the motor racing course?
4 Why/stop motor racing?
5 What/do next year?

Group B You are Sue. Make questions about Clem.

1 What/do when you were five?
2 When/do your first parachute jump?
2 Why /move to the country?
3 Why/love sky-diving?
4 What/do next July?

2 Work with a partner from the other group. Interview each other.

Clem Quinn
SKY-DIVER

Clem Quinn was always interested in flying. When he was five, he tried to fly by jumping off the garden shed with a golf umbrella, but when he grew up he didn't become a pilot, he became a taxi driver. Then 20 years ago he did a parachute jump and loved it. He decided that being a taxi driver in London was a lot more dangerous than jumping out of a plane, so he moved to the country to learn parachute jumping and sky-diving. He is now a full-time teacher of sky-diving. He says:

'I love sky-diving because the world looks so good – blue sky, green fields, white clouds. You float through the air, it's like floating in water. You can see forever, all the way to the French coast. The views are fantastic. You can forget all your worries. People think it is dangerous but it's very safe. Football is much more dangerous. Footballers often have accidents. When did you last hear of a sky-diving accident? Next July I'm going to do a sky-dive with 100 people from six planes. That's a record. I'm never going to retire. I'm going to jump out of planes until I'm an old man.'

Sue Glass

RACING DRIVER

Sue Glass had a car accident when she was eight so she didn't like driving. When she grew up this was a problem, because she got a job with a car company. Then six years ago she met Julian Swayland, a racing driver, and she told him she was afraid of cars. He wanted to help, so he took her to Brands Hatch, a Grand Prix racing circuit. He drove her round corners at 100 mph and she loved it. Then she heard about a special motor racing course. She did the course with five men and was amazed when she got top marks. She says:

'I think I did well because I listened to everything the teacher said. I needed to because I was so afraid. The men often didn't listen. The best moment was my first championship race. I didn't win but I came fourth. I beat 20 men. I love the excitement of motor racing but it's a dangerous sport and I'm always very frightened. In fact I stopped doing it a year ago, because I got so nervous before each race, I felt really sick. I'm not going to race again, I'm going to teach other people to drive. I'm going to open a driving school next year.'

VOCABULARY AND SPEAKING
The weather

1 Match the words and symbols.

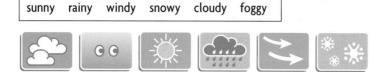

| sunny | rainy | windy | snowy | cloudy | foggy |

Which symbols can the following adjectives go with?

hot   warm   cold   cool   wet   dry

2 **T 12.6** Listen and complete the answers.

'What's the weather like today?' 'It's _____ and _____.'

'What was it like yesterday?' 'Oh, it was _____ and _____.'

'What's it going to be like tomorrow?' 'I think it's going to be _____.'

> **!** The question *What . . . like?* asks for a description.
> *What's the weather like?* = Tell me about the weather.

Practise the questions and answers. Ask and answer about the weather where *you* are today, yesterday, and tomorrow.

3 Work with a partner. Find out about the weather round the world yesterday.

Student A Look at the information on this page.
Student B Look at the information from your teacher.

Ask and answer questions to complete the information.

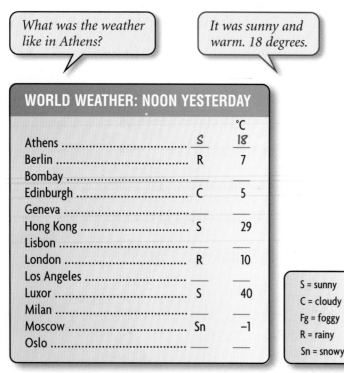

> *What was the weather like in Athens?*

> *It was sunny and warm. 18 degrees.*

WORLD WEATHER: NOON YESTERDAY

		°C
Athens	S	18
Berlin	R	7
Bombay	—	—
Edinburgh	C	5
Geneva	—	—
Hong Kong	S	29
Lisbon	—	—
London	R	10
Los Angeles	—	—
Luxor	S	40
Milan	—	—
Moscow	Sn	–1
Oslo	—	—

S = sunny
C = cloudy
Fg = foggy
R = rainy
Sn = snowy

4 Which city was the hottest? Which was the coldest?
Which month do you think it is?

EVERYDAY ENGLISH

Making suggestions

1 Make a list of things you can do in good weather and things you can do in bad weather. Compare your list with a partner.

Good weather	Bad weather
go to the beach	watch TV

2 **T 12.7** Read and listen to the beginning of two conversations. Complete **B**'s suggestions.

1 **A** It's a lovely day!
  What shall we do?
  B Let's _____ !

2 **A** It's raining again!
  What shall we do?
  B Let's _____ and _____ .

> ❗ 1 We use *shall* to ask for and make suggestions.
>   What shall we do?
>   Shall we go swimming? = I suggest that we go swimming.
>   2 We use *Let's* to make a suggestion for everyone.
>   Let's go! = I suggest that we all go. (Let's = Let us)
>   Let's have a pizza!

3 Match these lines with the two conversations in exercise 2. Put them in the correct order to complete the conversations.

Well, let's go to the beach.
OK. Which film do you want to see?
Oh no! It's too hot to play tennis.

Oh no! We watched a video last night.
OK. I'll get my swimming costume.
Well, let's go to the cinema.

T 12.8 Listen and check. Practise the conversations with your partner.

4 Have more conversations suggesting what to do when the weather is good or bad. Use your lists of activities in exercise 1 to help you.

13 How terribly clever!

Question forms · Adverbs and adjectives · Describing feelings · Catching a train

STARTER

1 Match a question word with an answer.

2 Look at the answers. What do you think the story is?

When . . . ?	Six.
Where . . . ?	1991.
What . . . ?	Paris.
Who . . . ?	Because I love him.
Why . . . ?	John.
Which . . . ?	Some roses.
How . . . ?	£25.
How much . . . ?	The red ones.
How many . . . ?	By plane.

A QUIZ
Question words

1 Work in groups and answer the quiz.

2 **T 13.1** Listen and check your answers. Listen carefully to the intonation of the questions.

GRAMMAR SPOT

1 Underline all the question words in the quiz.

2 Make *two* questions for each of these statements, one with a question word and one without.

> I live in London. (where)
> *'Where do you live?' 'In London.'*
> *'Do you live in London?' 'Yes, I do.'*

1 She's wearing jeans. (what)
2 She works in the bank. (where)
3 He's leaving tomorrow. (when)
4 I visited my aunt. (who)
5 We came by taxi. (how)
6 They're going to have a party. (why)

3 What are the short answers to the questions?

▶▶ **Grammar Reference 13.1 p124**

---

3 In groups, write some general knowledge questions. Ask the class!

GENERAL KN

1 When did the first man walk on the moon?
   a 1961   **b** 1965   **c** 1969

2 Where are the Andes mountains?

3 Who did Mother Teresa look after?

4 Who won the last World Cup?

5 How many American states are there?

6 How much does an African elephant weigh?
   a 3–5 tonnes   **b** 5–7 tonnes   **c** 7–9 tonnes

7 How far is it from London to New York?

   a 6,000 kilometres

   b 9,000 kilometres

   c 12,000 kilometres

PRACTICE

Questions and answers

1 Look at the question words in **A** and the answers in **C**. Choose the correct question from **B**.

A	B	C
Where		To the shops.
What		A new jacket.
When	did you buy?	This morning.
Who	did you go?	A friend from work.
Why	did you go with?	To buy some new clothes.
Which one	did you pay?	The black, leather one.
How		We drove.
How much		£120.99.
How many		Only one.

OWLEDGE QUIZ

8 How old was Princess Diana when she died?
a 33   **b** 36   **c** 39

9 What languages do Swiss people speak?

10 What did Marconi invent in 1901?

11 What sort of music did Louis Armstrong play?
a Jazz   **b** Blues   **c** Rock 'n' roll

12 What happens at the end of Romeo and Juliet?

13 What happened in Europe in 1939?

14 Why do birds migrate?

15 Which was the first country to have TV?
a Britain   **b** the USA   **c** Russia

16 Which language has the most words?
a French   **b** Chinese   **c** English

Listening and pronunciation

2 **T 13.2** Tick (✓) the sentence you hear.

1 ☐ Where do you want to go?
  ☐ Why do you want to go?

2 ☐ How is she?
  ☐ Who is she?

3 ☐ Where's he staying?
  ☐ Where's she staying?

4 ☐ Why did they come?
  ☐ Why didn't they come?

5 ☐ How old was she?
  ☐ How old is she?

6 ☐ Does he play the guitar?
  ☐ Did he play the guitar?

7 ☐ Where did you go at the weekend?
  ☐ Where do you go at the weekend?

Asking about you

3 Put the words in the correct order to make questions.

1 like learning do English you?
_____

2 do you night what did last?
_____

3 languages mother many does how your speak?
_____

4 last go you shopping did when?
_____

5 football which you do team support?
_____

6 come car today school by you to did?
_____

7 much do weigh you how?
_____

8 usually who sit you do next class in to?
_____

9 English want learn to you do why?
_____

4 Work with a partner. Ask and answer the questions.

DO IT CAREFULLY!
Adverbs and adjectives

1 Are the words in *italics* adjectives or adverbs?

1 Smoking is a *bad* habit.
  The team played *badly* and lost the match.
2 Please listen *carefully*.
  Jane's a *careful* driver.
3 The homework was *easy*.
  Peter's very good at tennis. He won the game *easily*.
4 I know the Prime Minister *well*.
  My husband's a *good* cook.
5 It's a *hard* life.
  Teachers work *hard* and don't earn much money.

> ## GRAMMAR SPOT
>
> **1** Look at these sentences.
>   Lunch is a quick meal for many people.
>   (*quick* = adjective. It describes a noun.)
>   I ate my lunch quickly.
>   (*quickly* = adverb. It describes a verb.)
>
> **2** How do we make regular adverbs? What happens when the adjective ends in *-y*?
>
> **3** There are two irregular adverbs in exercise 1. Find them.
>
> ▶▶ **Grammar Reference 13.2 p124**

2 Match the verbs or phrases with an adverb. Usually more than one answer is possible. Which are the irregular adverbs?

get up	slowly
walk	quietly
work	early
run	fluently
speak	carefully
speak English	easily
pass the exam	hard
do your homework	fast/quickly

PRACTICE

Order of adjectives/adverbs

1 Put the adjective in brackets in the correct place in the sentence. Where necessary, change the adjective to an adverb.

1 We had a holiday in Spain, but unfortunately we had weather. (terrible)
2 Maria dances. (good)
3 When I saw the accident, I phoned the police. (immediate)
4 Don't worry. Justin is a driver. (careful)
5 Jean-Pierre is a Frenchman. He loves food, wine, and rugby. (typical)
6 Please speak. I can't understand you. (slow)
7 We had a test today. (easy)
8 We all passed. (easy)
9 You speak English. (good)

Telling a story

2 Complete these sentences in a suitable way.

1 It started to rain. **Fortunately** …
2 Peter invited me to his party. **Unfortunately** …
3 I was fast asleep when **suddenly** …
4 I saw a man with a gun outside the bank. **Immediately** …

3 🔲**T 13.3** Look at the picture and listen to a man describing what happened to him in the middle of the night. Number the adverbs in the order you hear them.

☐ quickly
☐ quietly
☐ slowly
☐ immediately
☐ carefully
☐ suddenly
☐ fortunately
☐ really

4 Work with a partner and tell the story again. Use the order of the adverbs to help you.

Check it

5 Each sentence has a mistake. Find it and correct it.

1 Where does live Anna's sister?
2 The children came into the classroom noisyly.
3 What means *whistle*?
4 I always work hardly.
5 Do you can help me, please?
6 When is going Peter on holiday?

VOCABULARY
Describing feelings

1 Match the feelings to the pictures.

bored   tired   worried   excited   annoyed   interested

2 Match the feelings and reasons to make sentences.

	Feelings		Reasons
I am	bored tired worried excited annoyed interested	because	I'm going on holiday tomorrow. we have a good teacher. I worked very hard today. I can't find my keys. I have nothing to do. I want to go to the party but I can't.

> **!** Some adjectives can end in both *-ed* and *-ing*.
>
> The book was <u>interesting</u>.
> I was <u>interested</u> in the book.
> The lesson was <u>boring</u>.
> The students were <u>bored</u>.

3 Complete each sentence with the correct adjective.

1 **excited, exciting**
   Life in New York is very …
   The football fans were very …

2 **tired, tiring**
   The marathon runners were very …
   That game of tennis was very …

3 **annoyed, annoying**
   The child's behaviour was really …
   The teacher was … when nobody did the homework.

4 **worried, worrying**
   The news is very …
   Everybody was very … when they heard the news.

4 Answer your teacher's questions using adjectives from exercises 1 and 2.

Did you like doing exercise 2?

No, we didn't. It was very boring!

How did you feel?

Very bored!

READING AND LISTENING
A story in a story

1 Think about when you were a small child. Did your parents tell you stories? Which was your favourite story? Tell the class.

2 Look at the first picture. Who do you think the people on the train are? Do they know each other?

3 **T 13.4** Read and listen to part one of the story.

4 Answer the questions.

1 Who are the people on the train?
2 What does Cyril ask questions about?
3 Why does the aunt tell the children a story?
4 What is the story about?
5 Do the children like the story?
6 Why does the young man start speaking?
7 Which of these adjectives best describe the people? Write them in the correct column.

quiet noisy badly-behaved tired worried bored boring annoyed annoying

The aunt

The children

The young man

A TRAIN JOURNEY

The people on the train were hot and tired. A tall young man sat next to three small children and their aunt. The aunt and the children talked. When the aunt spoke she always began with 'Don't … '. When the children spoke they always began with 'Why … ?' The young man said nothing.

The small boy whistled loudly. 'Don't do that, Cyril,' said his aunt. Cyril stood up and looked out of the window at the countryside.
'Why is that man taking those sheep out of that field?' he asked.
'Perhaps he's taking them to another field where there's more grass,' said the aunt.
'But there's lots of grass in that field. Why can't the sheep stay there?'

73

'Perhaps the grass in the other field is better.'
'Why is it better?'
The young man looked annoyed.
'Oh dear,' thought the aunt, 'he doesn't like children.'
'Sit down quietly, Cyril. Now, listen, I'm going to tell you all a story.'

The children looked bored but they listened. The story was very boring indeed. It was about a very beautiful little girl, who worked hard and behaved beautifully. Everybody loved her. One day she fell into a lake and everyone in the village ran to save her.

'Why did they save her?' asked the bigger girl.
'Because she was so good,' said the aunt.
'But that's stupid,' said the girl. 'When people fall into lakes, it doesn't matter if they're good or bad, you run to save them.'
'You're right,' said the young man, speaking for the first time. 'That's a ridiculous story.'
'Well, perhaps *you* would like to tell a story,' said the aunt coldly.
'OK,' said the man. The children looked interested and he began.

5 The young man tells the story of a little girl called Bertha. Look at the pictures. What do you think happened to Bertha?

6 **T 13.5** Read and listen to part two.

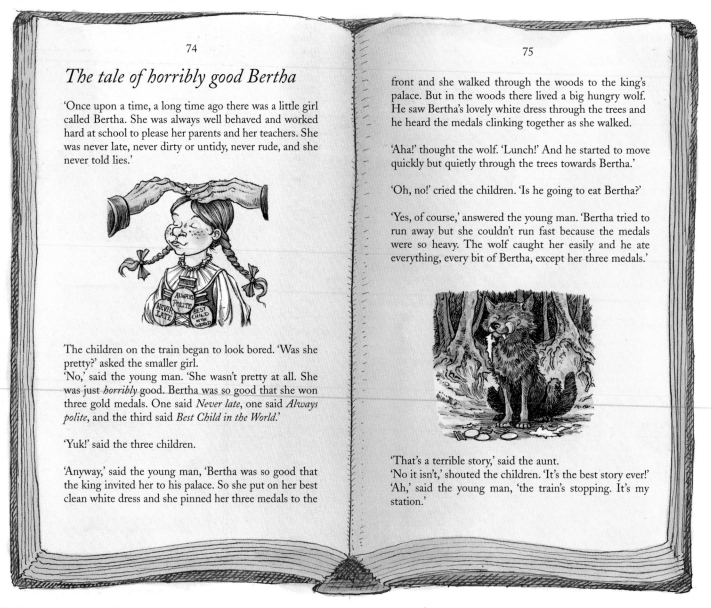

The tale of horribly good Bertha

'Once upon a time, a long time ago there was a little girl called Bertha. She was always well behaved and worked hard at school to please her parents and her teachers. She was never late, never dirty or untidy, never rude, and she never told lies.'

The children on the train began to look bored. 'Was she pretty?' asked the smaller girl.
'No,' said the young man. 'She wasn't pretty at all. She was just *horribly* good. Bertha was so good that she won three gold medals. One said *Never late*, one said *Always polite*, and the third said *Best Child in the World*.'

'Yuk!' said the three children.

'Anyway,' said the young man, 'Bertha was so good that the king invited her to his palace. So she put on her best clean white dress and she pinned her three medals to the

front and she walked through the woods to the king's palace. But in the woods there lived a big hungry wolf. He saw Bertha's lovely white dress through the trees and he heard the medals clinking together as she walked.

'Aha!' thought the wolf. 'Lunch!' And he started to move quickly but quietly through the trees towards Bertha.'

'Oh, no!' cried the children. 'Is he going to eat Bertha?'

'Yes, of course,' answered the young man. 'Bertha tried to run away but she couldn't run fast because the medals were so heavy. The wolf caught her easily and he ate everything, every bit of Bertha, except her three medals.'

'That's a terrible story,' said the aunt.
'No it isn't,' shouted the children. 'It's the best story ever!'
'Ah,' said the young man, 'the train's stopping. It's my station.'

74 / 75

7 Answer the questions.

1 What is the same and what is different in the aunt's story and the young man's story?
2 Does the aunt like the young man's story? Why/Why not?
3 Do the children like the story? Why/Why not?
4 Which of these do you think is the moral of Bertha's story?

> It pays to be good.
> It never pays to be good.
> It doesn't always pay to be good.

8 Tell the story of Bertha. Use the pictures in exercise 5 on p103 to help you.

Language work

1 Put some adjectives and adverbs from the story of Bertha into the correct box.

Adjectives	Adverbs

2 Write questions about Bertha's story using these question words. Ask and answer the questions across the class.

> ~~when~~ how many   what   why   where   how

> *When did the story take place?*   *A long time ago.*

EVERYDAY ENGLISH
Catching a train

1 Ann is phoning to find out the times of trains to Bristol.

T 13.6 Listen and write in the arrival times.

> **!** Notice we often use the twenty-four hour clock for timetables.
> 7.00 in the morning = 0700 (oh seven hundred hours)

2 **T 13.7** Ann is at Oxford Station. Listen and complete the conversation. Then practise with a partner.

A Good morning. (1) _____ the times of trains (2) _____ Bristol (3) _____ Oxford, please?

B Afternoon, evening? When (4) _____ ?

A About five o'clock this afternoon.

B About (5) _____ . Right. Let's have a look. There's a train that (6) _____ 5.28, then there isn't (7) _____ until 6.50.

A And (8) _____ get in?

B The 5.28 gets into Oxford at 6.54 and the 6.50 (9) _____ .

A Thanks a lot.

3 Ann goes to the ticket office. Put the lines of the conversation in the correct order.

- [1] **A** Hello. A return to Bristol, please.
- [ ] **A** A day return.
- [ ] **C** How do you want to pay?
- [11] **A** OK, thanks very much. Goodbye.
- [ ] **C** Here's your change and your ticket.
- [ ] **C** You want platform 1 over there.
- [ ] **A** Here's a twenty-pound note.
- [ ] **C** Day return or period return?
- [ ] **A** Cash, please.
- [ ] **C** That's eighteen pounds.
- [ ] **A** Thank you. Which platform is it?

T 13.8 Listen and check. Practise the conversation with a partner.

4 Make more conversations with your partner. Look at the information from your teacher. Decide where you want to go. Find out about times, then buy your ticket.

DEPARTURE TIME from OXFORD	ARRIVAL TIME at Bristol Temple Meads
0816	
0945	
1040	

Trains

14 Have you ever?

Present Perfect + *ever*, *never*, *yet*, and *just* · At the airport

STARTER

1 Match the countries and flags.

Australia	Brazil	France	Germany	Great Britain
Greece	Hungary	Italy	Japan	Canada	Spain	the USA

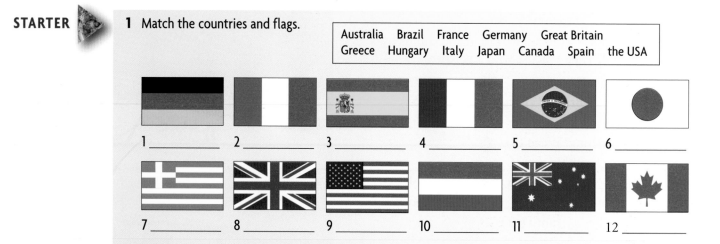

1 _____ 2 _____ 3 _____ 4 _____ 5 _____ 6 _____

7 _____ 8 _____ 9 _____ 10 _____ 11 _____ 12 _____

2 Tick (✓) the countries that you have visited.

IN MY LIFE
Present Perfect + *ever* and *never*

1 **T 14.1** Read and listen to the sentences. Then listen and repeat.

I've been to Germany. (I've = I have)
I haven't been to France.
I've been to the USA.
I've never been to Australia.
I haven't been to any of the countries!

Work in groups. Tell each other which of the countries above you have or haven't been to. Have you been to any other countries?

2 **T 14.2** Read and listen to the conversation. Practise with a partner.

A Have you ever been to Paris?
B No, I haven't.
A Have you ever been to Berlin?
B Yes, I have.
A When did you go?
B Two years ago.

Postcard text:

EL CAPITAN — SUNSET
YOSEMITE NATIONAL PARK, CALIFORNIA
Rising over 3,245 feet above the valley floor, El Capitan is one of the largest exposed monoliths in the world.
© Photograph by Chris Loberg

Hi guys!
San Francisco is fantastic! We are having a superb time - and are trying to see all the sights. We're staying near the Yosemite National Park, which is just beautiful.
See you guys soon (probably read this with you actually!)
Nicky

MELBOURNE AUSTRALIA

The weather is fantastic. We went to an Aussie football match yesterday and are off to a winery & then a 'barbie' tomorrow.

Le Moulin Rouge

BUDAPEST

LISBOA

PARIS

3 Write down the names of four cities in your country or another country that you have been to. Have similar conversations with your partner.

4 Tell the class about your partner.

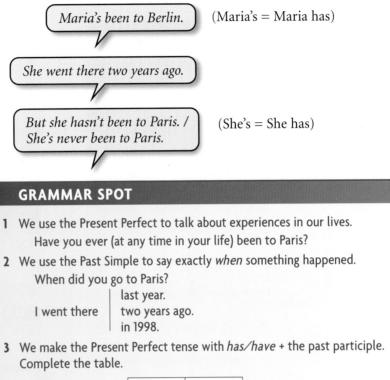

Maria's been to Berlin.   (Maria's = Maria has)

She went there two years ago.

But she hasn't been to Paris. / She's never been to Paris.   (She's = She has)

GRAMMAR SPOT

1 We use the Present Perfect to talk about experiences in our lives.
Have you ever (at any time in your life) been to Paris?

2 We use the Past Simple to say exactly *when* something happened.
When did you go to Paris?

I went there	last year. two years ago. in 1998.

3 We make the Present Perfect tense with *has/have* + the past participle. Complete the table.

	Positive	Negative	
I/You/We/They	_____	_____	been to Paris.
He/She/It	_____	_____	

4 Write *ever* and *never* in the right place in these sentences.
Has he _____ been to London?
He's _____ been to London.

▶▶ **Grammar Reference 14.1 p125**

PRACTICE

Past participles

1 Here are the past participles of some verbs. Write the infinitive.

eaten	**eat**	made	_____	given	_____
seen	_____	taken	_____	won	_____
met	_____	driven	_____	had	_____
drunk	_____	cooked	_____	stayed	_____
flown	_____	bought	_____	done	_____

2 Which are the two regular verbs?

3 What are the Past Simple forms of the verbs?

4 Look at the list of irregular verbs on p130 and check your answers.

The life of Ryan

1 **T 14.3** Listen to Ryan talking about his life and tick (✓) the things he has done.

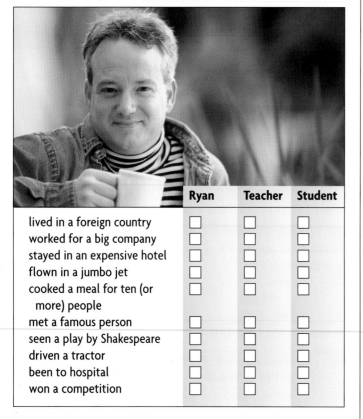

	Ryan	Teacher	Student
lived in a foreign country	☐	☐	☐
worked for a big company	☐	☐	☐
stayed in an expensive hotel	☐	☐	☐
flown in a jumbo jet	☐	☐	☐
cooked a meal for ten (or more) people	☐	☐	☐
met a famous person	☐	☐	☐
seen a play by Shakespeare	☐	☐	☐
driven a tractor	☐	☐	☐
been to hospital	☐	☐	☐
won a competition	☐	☐	☐

2 Tell your teacher about Ryan and answer your teacher's questions.

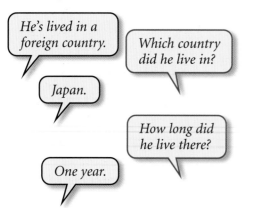

> *He's lived in a foreign country.*
>
> *Which country did he live in?*
>
> *Japan.*
>
> *How long did he live there?*
>
> *One year.*

3 Ask your teacher the questions and complete the chart.

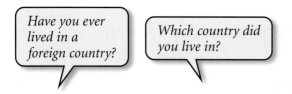

> *Have you ever lived in a foreign country?*
>
> *Which country did you live in?*

4 Ask a partner the questions. Tell the class about your partner.

A HONEYMOON IN LONDON
Present Perfect + *yet* and *just*

1 Rod and Marilyn come from Christchurch, New Zealand. They are on honeymoon in London. Before they went, they made a list of things they wanted to do there. Read the list below.

2 **T 14.4** Marilyn is phoning her sister Judy, back home in New Zealand. Listen to their conversation. Tick (✓) the things she and Rod have done.

LONDON

Things to do –
- go to Buckingham Palace
- see the Houses of Parliament
- have a boat ride on the River Thames
- go on the London Eye
- walk in Hyde Park
- go shopping in Harrods
- see the Crown Jewels in the Tower of London
- travel on a double-decker bus
- go to the theatre

GRAMMAR SPOT

1 Complete the sentences.
  1 Have you _____ the Crown Jewels **yet**?
  2 We _____ been to the theatre **yet**.
  3 We've **just** _____ a boat ride on the Thames.

2 Where do we put *yet* in a sentence? Where do we put *just* in a sentence?

3 We can only use *yet* with **two** of the following. Which two?
  ☐ Positive sentences
  ☐ Questions
  ☐ Negative sentences

▶▶ **Grammar Reference 14.2 p125**

3 Look at the list with a partner. Say what Rod and Marilyn have done and what they haven't done yet.

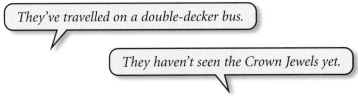

They've travelled on a double-decker bus.

They haven't seen the Crown Jewels yet.

T 14.4 Listen again and check.

PRACTICE

I've just done it

1 Work with a partner. Make questions with *yet* and answers with *just*.

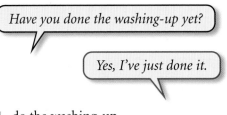

Have you done the washing-up yet?

Yes, I've just done it.

  1 do the washing-up
  2 do the shopping
  3 wash your hair
  4 clean the car
  5 make the dinner
  6 meet the new student
  7 have a coffee
  8 give your homework to the teacher
  9 finish the exercise

Check it

2 Tick (✓) the correct sentence.
  1 ☐ I saw John yesterday.
    ☐ I've seen John yesterday.
  2 ☐ Did you ever eat Chinese food?
    ☐ Have you ever eaten Chinese food?
  3 ☐ Donna won £5,000 last month.
    ☐ Donna has won £5,000 last month.
  4 ☐ I've never drank champagne.
    ☐ I've never drunk champagne.
  5 ☐ Tom has ever been to America.
    ☐ Tom has never been to America.
  6 ☐ Has your sister yet had the baby?
    ☐ Has your sister had the baby yet?
  7 ☐ I haven't finished my homework yet.
    ☐ I've finished my homework yet.
  8 ☐ Did she just bought a new car?
    ☐ Has she just bought a new car?

READING AND SPEAKING
How to live to be 100

1 Who is the oldest person you know? How old is he/she? What do you know about their lives? Why do you think they have lived so long? Tell the class.

2 These words are in the texts. Write them in the correct column.

pneumonia   ambulance driver   engineer   heart attack
lung cancer   rheumatic fever   secretary   dressmaker

Jobs	Illnesses

3 Read the introduction. Are similar facts true for your country?

How to live to be 100

More and more people are living to be 100 years old. There are now 4,400 centenarians in Britain – 10 times more than there were 40 years ago. Professor Grimley Evans of Oxford University believes that future generations will live even longer, to 115 years and more. Here are the stories of three people who have lived to be 100.

4 Work in groups of three. Each choose a different person and read about her/him. Answer the questions.

1 What jobs has she/he had in her/his life?
2 Where does he/she live now?
3 Which countries has she/he been to?
4 Did he/she marry and have children?
5 Is her husband/his wife still alive?
6 When and why did she/he give up smoking cigarettes?
7 What do you learn about other people in his/her family?
8 Has she/he ever been very ill?
9 What food does he/she like?
10 What exercise does she/he like doing?

5 Work with your group. Compare the three people, using your answers.

What do you think?

• Why do you think these people have lived so long? How many reasons can you find?
• Would you like to live to be 100? Why/why not?

Joyce Bews

Joyce Bews was 100 last year. She was born and grew up in Portsmouth on the south coast of England, where she still lives. For many years she was a dressmaker, and she didn't marry until she was 65. Her husband died of lung cancer only 10 weeks after they married. It was then that she gave up smoking. Joyce has had only one serious illness in her life – she had pneumonia when she was 20. She has lived in Australia and America. She lived in Australia after her husband died, and she went to America when she was 75. She has just returned from a holiday in Spain with her niece, aged 75. She says: 'I'm not sure why I've lived so long. I've never exercised but I've always eaten well, lots of fruit. My youngest brother has just died, aged 90.'

Alice Patterson-Smythe

Alice Patterson-Smythe was born just over 100 years ago in Edinburgh. She now lives in Norfolk. She drove ambulances in the First World War, and worked as a school secretary until she retired. She has been a widow for 25 years and has three children, six grandchildren, and 11 great-grandchildren. She smoked quite a lot when she was a young girl but she gave up when she was 68 because she had a heart attack. Her nineties were the best years of her life because her millionaire grandson took her on his aeroplane to visit Tokyo, Los Angeles, and Miami. She says: 'I love life. I play golf once a week and do Latin American dancing, and I eat lots of fruit and vegetables. We are a long-lived family – my mother was 95 when she died.'

Tommy Harrison

Tommy Harrison is exactly 100 years old. He's a retired engineer. His wife, Maude, died 14 years ago. They had no children and now he lives alone in his flat in Bristol. Tommy has smoked all his life. First he smoked cigarettes, about 10 a day, but 40 years ago he changed to a pipe. He has only been ill once in his life, and that was just before the First World War, when he had rheumatic fever. The only time he visits his doctor is to get a certificate to say that he can still drive his car. Every day he has a full English breakfast – bacon, eggs, toast and marmalade. He has only been abroad once, to France during the war. He says: 'I still go dancing and swimming but I don't want to live for ever, perhaps 12 more months. My father lived until he was 99.'

LISTENING
Leaving on a jet plane

1 **T 14.5** Close your books and your eyes and listen to a song. What is it about?

2 Read the words of the song. Choose the word on the right which best completes the line.

Leaving on a jet plane

My (1)_____ are packed, I'm ready to go,
I'm standing here outside your (2)_____ ,
I (3)_____ to wake you up to say goodbye,
But the dawn is breaking,
It's early morn',
The taxi's (4)_____ ,
he's blowing his (5)_____ ,
Already I'm so lonesome
I could (6)_____ .

1	bags suitcases
2	window door
3	hate want
4	here waiting
5	horn trumpet
6	cry die

Chorus   So kiss me and (7)_____ for me,
(8)_____ me that you'll wait for me,
(9)_____ me like you'll never let me go,
'Cos I'm leaving on a jet plane,
I don't know when I'll be back again.
Oh babe, I hate to go.

7	laugh smile
8	tell say
9	love hold

There's so (10)_____ times I've let you down,
So many times I've (11)_____ around,
I tell you now
They don't mean a thing.
Every (12)_____ I go, I'll think of you
Every song I sing, I'll sing for you
When I (13)_____ back
I'll wear your wedding (14)_____ .

10	much many
11	played walked
12	time place
13	come go
14	ring dress

3 Listen again and check the words. Sing along!

EVERYDAY ENGLISH
At the airport

1 What do you do at an airport? Read the sentences and put them in the correct order.

- ☐ You wait in the departure lounge.
- ☐ You board the plane.
- ☐ You get a trolley for your luggage.
- ☑ You arrive at the airport.
- ☐ You check in your luggage and get a boarding pass.
- ☐ You go through passport control.
- ☐ You check the departures board for your gate number.

2 **T 14.6** Listen to the airport announcements and complete the chart.

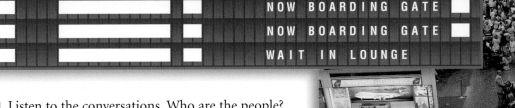

FLIGHT NUMBER	DESTINATION	GATE NUMBER	REMARK
B A 5 1 6	G E N E V A	4	L A S T C A L L
S K ____	____	____	D E L A Y E D ____
A F ____	____	____	N O W B O A R D I N G G A T E ____
L H ____	____	____	N O W B O A R D I N G G A T E ____
V S ____	____	____	W A I T I N L O U N G E

3 **T 14.7** Listen to the conversations. Who are the people? Where are they? Choose from these places.

- in the arrival hall
- in the departure lounge
- at the departure gate
- at the check-in desk

4 Complete each conversation with the correct question.

> When can we see each other again?
> Did you have a good honeymoon?
> Did the announcement say gate 4 or 14?
> have you got much hand luggage?

1 **A** Listen! … BA 516 to Geneva. That's our flight.
  B _____ ?
  A I couldn't hear. I think it said 4.
  B Look! There it is on the departure board. It *is* gate 4.
  A OK. Come on! Let's go.

2 **A** Can I have your ticket, please?
  B Yes, of course.
  A Thank you. How many suitcases have you got?
  B Just one.
  A And _____ ?
  B Just this bag.
  A That's fine.
  B Oh … can I have a seat next to the window?
  A Yes, that's OK. Here's your boarding pass. Have a nice flight!

  T 14.7 Listen and check. Practise the conversations with a partner.

3 **A** Rod! Marilyn! Over here!
  B Hi! Judy! Great to see you!
  A It's great to see you too. You look terrific!
  _____ ?
  B Fantastic. Everything was fantastic.
  A Well, you haven't missed anything here. Nothing much has happened at all!

4 **A** There's my flight. It's time to go.
  B Oh no! It's been a wonderful two weeks. I can't believe it's over.
  A I know. _____ ?
  B Soon, I hope. I'll write every day.
  A I'll phone too. Goodbye.
  B Goodbye. Give my love to your family.

5 Work with a partner. Make more conversations at each of the places.

Tapescripts

Unit 8

T 8.1 **Inventions**

JEANS

Two Americans, Jacob Davis and Levi Strauss, made the first jeans in 1873. Davis bought cloth from Levi's shop. He told Levi that he had a special way to make strong trousers for workmen. The first jeans were blue. In 1935 jeans became fashionable for women after they saw them in *Vogue* magazine. In the 1970s, Calvin Klein earned $12.5 million a week from jeans.

TELEVISION

A Scotsman, John Logie Baird, transmitted the first television picture on 25 October, 1925. The first thing on television was a boy who worked in the office next to Baird's workroom in London. In 1927 Baird sent pictures from London to Glasgow. In 1928 he sent pictures to New York, and also produced the first colour TV pictures.

ASPIRIN

Felix Hofman a 29-year-old chemist who worked for the German company Bayer, invented the drug Aspirin in March 1899. He gave the first aspirin to his father for his arthritis. By 1950 it was the best-selling painkiller in the world and in 1969 the Apollo astronauts took it to the moon. The Spanish philosopher, José Ortega y Gasset, called the 20th century 'The Age of Aspirin'.

T 8.2 **Negatives and positives**

1 Two Germans didn't make the first jeans. Two Americans made them.
2 Davis didn't sell cloth in Levi's shop. He bought cloth from Levi's shop.
3 Women didn't see pictures of jeans in *She* magazine. They saw them in *Vogue*.
4 Baird didn't send pictures from London to Paris. He sent pictures from London to Glasgow.
5 Felix Hofman didn't give the first aspirin to his mother. He gave it to his father.
6 A Spanish philosopher didn't call the 19th century, 'the Age of Aspirin'. He called the 20th century, 'the Age of Aspirin'.

T 8.3 see p62

T 8.4 **Listen and repeat**

1	recipe	6	worried
2	chat	7	delicious
3	shy	8	sandwich
4	funny	9	machine
5	face	10	century

T 8.5 **Everyday conversations**

1 **A** Why didn't you laugh at my joke?
   B Because it wasn't very funny. That's why!

2 **A** Hello. Hello. I can't hear you. Who is it?
   B It's me, Jonathon … JONATHON! I'm on my mobile phone.
   A Oh, Jonathon! Hi! Sorry, I can't chat now. I'm in a hurry.

3 **A** Good luck in your exams!
   B Oh, thank you. I always get so nervous before exams.

4 **A** Mmmmm! Did you make this chocolate cake?
   B I did. Do you like it?
   A Like it? I love it. It's delicious. Can I have the recipe?

5 **A** Come on, Tommy. Say hello to Auntie Mavis. Don't be shy.
   B Hello, Auntie Mavis.

T 8.6

Love on the Internet – Debbie and Per

Debbie I'm really quite shy. I find it difficult to talk to people face to face. But I find it easy to chat on the Internet. I met Per there about a year ago. It was on a chatline called 'the Chat Room'. He was so funny.

Per But I'm only funny on the Internet! Anyway, we 'chatted' on the Internet for a year, we exchanged hundreds of e-mails and some photographs. I wanted to phone Debbie but …

Debbie I said no. I was worried. I didn't want it to end.

Per She didn't even give me her address. But finally she said OK, I could phone, so I did, and we spoke for an hour. It was very expensive! That was six months ago. Then she sent me her address and …

Debbie … that was three months ago and one week later, there was a knock at the door and I knew before I opened it. Somehow I wasn't worried any more. I opened the door and …

Per … and I stood there with some flowers …

Debbie … lots of flowers. Red roses. Beautiful … and …

Per … and well, we fell in love and …

Both … and we got married last Saturday.

Love in a bottle – Rosa and Vincent

Rosa I love the sea. I like walking on the beach. One day, it was five years ago now, I was on the beach and I stood on something, it was a bottle, a green bottle. I could see something inside. Some paper, so I broke the bottle, it was a letter but …

Vincent … but you couldn't read it …

Rosa No, I couldn't. You see it was in English and I couldn't speak English then.

Vincent You can speak it well now …

Rosa No, not really, but anyway. I asked a friend to translate the letter for me. We couldn't believe it. A man in America – he wanted a wife, but the letter was ten years old.

Vincent And I still wasn't married!

Rosa But I didn't know that. Anyway for a joke I wrote and sent a photo …

Vincent And now, I couldn't believe it. I got this letter and a photo. She looked beautiful. I wrote back immediately and we wrote every week for six months … and we spoke on the phone and …

Rosa … and finally I flew to America and we met face to face. I was very shy but it was good, very good and now …

Vincent … now, we have three children. We have a house by the sea …

Rosa We're very happy. You see, we both love the sea!

T 8.7 **Ordinals**

first
second
third
fourth
fifth
sixth
tenth
twelfth
thirteenth
sixteenth
seventeenth
twentieth
twenty-first
thirtieth
thirty-first

T 8.8 **Dates**

1 The first of April
   April the first
2 The second of March
   March the second
3 The seventeenth of September
   September the seventeenth
4 The nineteenth of November
   November the nineteenth
5 The twenty-third of June

June the twenty-third
6 The twenty-ninth of February, nineteen seventy-six
7 The nineteenth of December, nineteen eighty-three
8 The third of October, nineteen ninety-nine
9 The thirty-first of May, two thousand
10 The fifteenth of July, two thousand and four

T 8.9 What's the date?

1 The fourth of January
2 May the seventh, 1997
3 The fifteenth of August, 2001
4 A It was a Friday.
   B No, it wasn't. It was a Thursday.
   A No, I remember. It was Friday the thirteenth. The thirteenth of July.
5 A Oh no! I forgot your birthday.
   B It doesn't matter, really.
   A It was last Sunday, wasn't it? The thirtieth. November the thirtieth.
6 A Hey! Did you know that Shakespeare was born and died on the same day?
   B That's not possible!
   A Yes, it is. He was born on April the twenty-third, fifteen sixty-four and he died on April the twenty-third, sixteen sixteen.

Unit 9

T 9.1 Food you like

D = Daisy   T = Tom
D I don't like tea.
T Oh, I do. Well, sometimes, with sugar. But coffee's horrible!
D Yeah. Disgusting. I don't like wine or beer either.
T Well – I don't like wine but I like beer. My dad has beer every day after work and sometimes I have a bit.
D Beer! Yuk! But apple juice is nice. I really like apple juice. It's delicious.
T Mmmm! Yeah, it's delicious and it's good for you. Apples are too! I love all fruit – apples, oranges, bananas, strawberries.
D Yeah. OK. I like fruit, but I hate all vegetables, 'specially carrots.
T Yeah, vegetables are disgusting. Eh – but not all of them, – I quite like peas. Hamburgers, chips, and peas. Mmm! That's one of my favourite meals.
D Yeah – hamburgers, I like. Chips, I like. But peas – yuk!
T My very favourite meal is spaghetti. Spaghetti, then ice-cream after. Yummy! … Or yoghurt. I love strawberry yoghurt.
D Ice-cream – OK, yes. Yoghurt, no! Spaghetti – yes. I like all pasta and pizza! But I don't like it with tomatoes or cheese. I don't like tomatoes very much and I hate cheese.
T Mmmm! Pizza. The best. But … you can't have pizza without tomatoes and cheese.

D You can.
T You can't!
D Can!
T Can't!
D Well, I can. I don't like cheese at all!
T What do you like then?
D Well, I like … er … I like chocolate and chocolate biscuits …
T Yeah! I really like chocolate. Everybody likes chocolate.
D Yeah!

T 9.2 see p67

T 9.3 Questions and answers

1 Would you like a cigarette?
  No, thanks. I don't smoke.

2 Do you like your teacher?
  Yes. She's very nice.

3 Would you like a drink?
  Yes, please. Some Coke, please.

4 Can I help you?
  Yes. I'd like a book of stamps, please.

5 What sports do you do?
  Well, I like swimming very much.

6 Excuse me, are you ready to order?
  Yes. I'd like a steak, please.

T 9.4 Listen carefully!

1 Good afternoon. Can I help you?
2 Who's your favourite writer?
3 What would you like for your birthday?
4 Do you like animals?
5 Here's the wine list, sir.
6 Have some ice-cream with your strawberries.

T 9.5

1 A Good afternoon. Can I help you?
  B Yes. I'd like some fruit, please.
2 A Who's your favourite writer?
  B I like books by John Grisham.
3 A What would you like for your birthday?
  B I'd like a new bike.
4 A Do you like animals?
  B I like cats, but I don't like dogs.
5 A Here's the wine list, sir.
  B We'd like a bottle of French red wine.
6 A Have some ice-cream with your strawberries.
  B No, thanks. I don't like ice-cream.

T 9.6 Going shopping

B = Barry   MP = Miss Potts
MP Good morning. Can I help you?
B Yes. I'd like some orange juice, please.
MP Er … sorry. There's apple juice but no orange juice.
B What's that then? Isn't that orange juice?
MP Oh, yes. So it is! My eyes! Here you are.
B Thank you, and some milk, please.
MP Sorry. I sold the last bottle two minutes ago.
B Oh, dear! What about some coffee?
MP Yes. Here you are.
B Thanks. That's orange juice, coffee … er … and … er … a kilo of apples, please.

MP I don't sell apples.
B You don't sell apples! That's strange. What about cheese. Can I have some cheese?
MP I don't sell cheese, either.
B You don't sell cheese! That's amazing. Now, I want some pizza, but I'm sure you don't sell pizza, do you?
MP Oh, yes I do. What would you like? Pizza with mushrooms, pizza with cheese and ham, pizza with sausage, or pizza with tomatoes?
B Wow! Can I have … er … some pizza with cheese and tomatoes, please?
MP Oh, sorry. I forgot. Usually, I have pizza but not on Thursdays. Today's Thursday, isn't it?
B Yes, it is. Mmm … OK, … er … OK, forget the pizza. What about bread? I don't suppose you have any bread?
MP Yes, you're right.
B Pardon?
MP You're right. There isn't any bread.
B Tell me. Do you do a lot of business?
MP Oh, yes sir. This shop is open 24 hours.
B Really! What do people buy?
MP All the things you see.
B Mmmm. OK. That's all for me. How much?
MP That's £5.60, please.
B Thank you. Goodbye.
MP Goodbye sir. See you again soon.
B I don't think so.

T 9.7 My favourite food

Marian
Well, I love vegetables, all vegetables – I eat meat too – but not much. I think this is why I like Chinese food so much. There are lots of vegetables in Chinese food. Yes, Chinese is my very favourite food, I like the noodles too. Can you eat with chopsticks? I can!

Graham
Now in my job, I travel the world, and I like all kinds of food … but my favourite, my favourite is … er … I always have it as soon as I come home … is a full English breakfast. Bacon, eggs, sausage, mushrooms, tomatoes, and of course toast. I love it, not every day but when I'm at home we have it every Sunday. Mmmm! I'd like it right now – delicious.

Lucy
Oh, no question, no problem. I know exactly what my favourite food is. Pasta. All pasta. Especially spaghetti. Pasta with tomato sauce – and I like it best when I'm in Italy. I went on holiday to the Italian lakes last year. The food was wonderful.

Gavin
… er … I'm not sure. No, I know what it is. My … favourite … food is Indian food. Friday night I like to go to the pub with friends from work and … have a few beers, … er … no, not too many, … and after we always go to an Indian restaurant and I have a chicken curry with rice. It's the best! I like it more than chips!

Sally

Well, shhh! But my very, very favourite food is chocolate. Chocolate anything, I love it. Chocolate ice-cream, chocolate biscuits, chocolate cake, but especially just a big bar of chocolate. Mmmm! Terrible, isn't it? Go on! Have some of this! My friend brought it back from Switzerland for me!

T 9.8 **Polite requests**

1 Would you like some more carrots?
   Yes, please. They're delicious.
2 Could you pass the salt, please?
   Yes, of course. Here you are.
3 Could I have a glass of water, please?
   Do you want fizzy or still?
4 Does anybody want more dessert?
   Yes, please. I'd love some. It's delicious.
5 How would you like your coffee?
   Black, no sugar, please.
6 This is delicious! Can you give me the recipe?
   Yes, of course. I'm glad you like it.
7 Do you want help with the washing-up?
   No, of course not. We have a dishwasher.

T 9.9

1 Can I have a cheese sandwich, please?
   Yes, of course. That's £1.75.
2 Could you tell me the time, please?
   It's just after ten.
3 Can you take me to school?
   Jump in.
4 Can I see the menu, please?
   Here you are. And would you like a drink to start?
5 Could you lend me some money, please?
   Not again! How much would you like this time?
6 Can you help me with my homework, please?
   What is it? French? I can't speak a word of French.
7 Can I borrow your dictionary, please?
   Yes, if I can find it. I think it's in my bag.

Unit 10

T 10.1 **Listen and repeat**

The country is cheaper and safer than the city.
The city is noisier and dirtier than the country.
The city is more expensive than the country.
The city is more exciting than the country.

T 10.2 **Much more than …**

1 A Life in the country is slower than city life.
   B Yes, the city's much faster.
2 A New York is safer than London.
   B No, it isn't. New York is much more dangerous.
3 A Paris is bigger than Madrid.
   B No, it isn't! It's much smaller.

4 A Madrid is more expensive than Rome.
   B No, it isn't. Madrid is much cheaper.
5 A The buildings in Rome are more modern than the buildings in New York.
   B No, they aren't. They're much older.
6 A The Underground in London is better than the Metro in Paris.
   B No! The Underground is much worse.

T 10.3 **Mel's got a better job**

Tara Why did you leave London? You had a good job.
Mel Yes, but I've got a better job here.
Tara And you had a big flat in London.
Mel Well, I've got a bigger flat here.
Tara Really? How many bedrooms has it got?
Mel Three. And it's got a garden. It's nicer than my flat in London and it's cheaper.
Tara But you haven't got any friends!
Mel I've got a lot of friends here. People are much friendlier than in London.
Tara But the country's so boring.
Mel No, it isn't. It's much more exciting than London. Seacombe has got shops, a cinema, a theatre, and a park. And the air is cleaner and the streets are safer.
Tara OK. Everything is wonderful! So when can I visit you?

T 10.4 **The biggest and best!**

1 That house is very big.
   Yes, it's the biggest house in the village.
2 Claridges is a very expensive hotel.
   Yes, it's the most expensive hotel in London.
3 Castle Combe is a very pretty village.
   Yes, it's the prettiest village in England.
4 New York is a very cosmopolitan city.
   Yes, it's the most cosmopolitan city in the world.
5 Tom Hanks is a very popular film star.
   Yes, he's the most popular film star in America.
6 Miss Smith is a very funny teacher.
   Yes, she's the funniest teacher in our school.
7 Anna is a very intelligent student.
   Yes, she's the most intelligent student in the class.
8 This is a very easy exercise.
   Yes, it's the easiest exercise in the book.

T 10.5 **Listen and respond**

1 That house is very big.
2 Claridges is a very expensive hotel.
3 Castle Combe is a very pretty village.
4 New York is a very cosmopolitan city.
5 Tom Hanks is a very popular film star.
6 Miss Smith is a very funny teacher.
7 Anna is a very intelligent student.
8 This is a very easy exercise.

T 10.6 **A musical interlude**

(three music exerpts)

T 10.7 **Listen and repeat**

wood
theatre
farm
village
factory
cottage
field
church

T 10.8 **To the lake**

Drive along Park Road and turn right. Go under the bridge and past the pub. Turn left up the hill, then drive down the hill to the river. Turn right after the farm and the lake is on the right. It takes twenty minutes.

T 10.9 **A drive in the country**

Well, I drove out of the garage, along the road, and under the bridge. Then I drove past the pub, up the hill, and down the hill. But then I drove over the river, and then – it was terrible – I went through the hedge, and into the lake!

Unit 11

T 11.1 **Who's at the party?**

O = Oliver   M = Monica

O Oh dear! Monica, I don't know any of these people. Who are they?
M Don't worry Oliver. They're all very nice. Can you see that man over there? He's sitting down. That's Harry. He's a musician. He works in LA.
O Sorry, where?
M You know, LA. Los Angeles.
O Oh yeah.
M And he's talking to Mandy. She's wearing a red dress. She's very nice and very rich! She lives in a beautiful old house in the country.
O Rich, eh?
M Yes. Rich and married! Next to her is Fiona. She's drinking a glass of red wine. Fiona's my oldest friend, she and I were at school together.
O And what does Fiona do?
M She's a writer. She writes children's stories – they're not very good but … anyway, she's talking to George. He's laughing and smoking a cigar. He's a pilot. He travels the world, thousands of miles every week.
O And who are those two over there? They're dancing. Mmmm. They know each other very well.
M Oh, that's Roz and Sam. They're married. They live in the flat upstairs.
O So … er … that's Harry and Mandy and … er … it's no good, I can't remember all those names.

T 11.2 Listen to the questions
1 Whose is the baseball cap?
2 Whose are the roller blades?
3 Whose is the dog?

T 11.3 *who's* or *whose*?
1 Who's on the phone?
2 I'm going to the pub. Who's coming?
3 Wow! Look at that sports car. Whose is it?
4 Whose dictionary is this? It's not mine.
5 There are books all over the floor. Whose are they?
6 Who's the most intelligent in our class?
7 Who's got my book?
8 Do you know whose jacket this is?

T 11.4 What a mess!
A Whose is this tennis racket?
B It's mine.
A What's it doing here?
B I'm playing tennis this afternoon.

T 11.5 What a wonderful world
I see trees of green
Red roses too
I see them bloom for me and you
And I think to myself
what a wonderful world.
I see skies of blue
and clouds of white
the bright sunny day
and the dark starry night
and I think to myself
what a wonderful world
The colours of the rainbow
so pretty in the sky
are also on the faces
of the people going by.
I see friends shaking hands
saying 'How do you do?'
They're really saying
'I love you.'
I hear babies cry
I watch them grow.
They'll learn much more
than you'll ever know
and I think to myself
what a wonderful world.
Yes, I think to myself
what a wonderful world.

T 11.6 Vowels and diphthongs
Vowels
1 red   said
2 hat   that
3 kissed   list
4 green   mean
5 laugh   half
6 whose   shoes
7 short   bought
Diphthongs
1 white   night
2 near   beer
3 they   pay
4 hair   wear
5 rose   knows
6 ours   flowers

T 11.7 Tongue twisters
1 Four fine fresh fish for you.
2 Six silly sisters selling shiny shoes.
3 If a dog chews shoes, whose shoes does he choose?
4 I'm looking back,
   To see if she's looking back,
   To see if I'm looking back,
   To see if she's looking back at me!

T 11.8 In a clothes shop
SA = shop assistant   C = customer
SA Can I help you?
C   Yes, please. I'm looking for a shirt to go with my new suit.
SA What colour are you looking for?
C   Blue.
SA What about this one? Do you like this?
C   No, it isn't the right blue.
SA Well, what about this one? It's a bit darker blue.
C   Oh yes. I like that one much better. Can I try it on?
SA Yes, of course. The changing rooms are over there.
    Is the size OK?
C   No, it's a bit too big. Have you got a smaller size?
SA That's the last blue one we've got, I'm afraid. But we've got it in white.
C   OK. I'll take the white. How much is it?
SA £39.99. How do you want to pay?
C   Can I pay by credit card?
SA Credit card's fine. Thank you very much.

Unit 12

T 12.1
Rosie
When I grow up I'm going to be a ballet dancer. I love dancing. I go dancing three times a week. I'm going to travel all over the world and I'm going to learn French and Russian because I want to dance in Paris and Moscow. I'm not going to marry until I'm thirty-five and then I'm going to have two children. First I'd like a girl and then a boy – but maybe I can't plan that! I'm going to work until I'm 75. I'm going to teach dancing and I'm going to open a dance school. It's all very exciting.

Miss Bishop
When I retire … ? … er … well … er … two things. First, I'm going to learn Russian – I can already speak French and German, and I want to learn another language. And second, I'm going to learn to drive. It's terrible that I'm 59 and I can't drive – no time to learn. Then I'm going to buy a car and travel all over the world. Also I'm not going to wear boring clothes any more, I hate the skirts and blouses I wear every day for school. I'm going to wear jeans and T-shirts all the time. And when I return from my travels I'm going to write a book and go on TV to talk about it. I'm going

to become a TV star!

T 12.2 Listen and repeat
A Is she going to be a ballet dancer?
B Yes, she is.
A What's she going to do?
B Travel all over the world.

T 12.3 Questions about Rosie
1 A Why is she going to learn French and Russian?
   B Because she wants to dance in Paris and Moscow.
2 A When is she going to marry?
   B Not until she's thirty-five.
3 A How many children is she going to have?
   B Two.
4 A How long is she going to work?
   B Until she's seventy-five.
5 A What is she going to teach?
   B Dancing.

T 12.4 It's going to rain
1 Take an umbrella. It's going to rain.
2 Look at the time! You're going to be late for the meeting.
3 Anna's running very fast. She's going to win the race.
4 Look! Jack's on the wall. He's going to fall.
5 Look at that man! He's going to jump.
6 They're going to have a baby. It's due next month.
7 There's my sister and her boyfriend! Yuk! They're going to kiss.
8 'Oh dear. I'm going to sneeze. Aaattishooo!'
   'Bless you!'

T 12.5 Why are you going?
MB = Miss Bishop   H = Harold
MB First I'm going to Holland.
H   Why?
MB To see the tulips, of course!
H   Oh yes! How wonderful! Where are you going after that?
MB Well, then I'm going to Spain to watch flamenco dancing.

T 12.6 The weather
A What's the weather like today?
B It's snowy and it's very cold.
A What was it like yesterday?
B Oh, it was cold and cloudy.
A What's it going to be like tomorrow?
B I think it's going to be warmer.

T 12.7 Conversations about the weather
1 A It's a lovely day! What shall we do?
   B Let's play tennis!
2 A It's raining again! What shall we do?
   B Let's stay at home and watch a video.

T 12.8

1 A It's a lovely day! What shall we do?
   B Let's play tennis!
   A Oh no! It's too hot to play tennis.
   B Well, let's go to the beach.
   A OK. I'll get my swimming costume.
2 A It's raining again! What shall we do?
   B Let's stay at home and watch a video.
   A Oh no! We watched a video last night.
   B Well, let's go to the cinema.
   A OK. Which film do you want to see?

Unit 13

T 13.1 A general knowledge quiz

1 When did the first man walk on the moon?
   In 1969.
2 Where are the Andes mountains?
   In South America.
3 Who did Mother Teresa look after?
   Poor people in Calcutta.
4 Who won the last World Cup?
   France in 1998.
5 How many American states are there?
   50.
6 How much does an African elephant weigh?
   5–7 tonnes.
7 How far is it from London to New York?
   6,000 kilometres.
8 How old was Princess Diana when she died?
   36.
9 What languages do Swiss people speak?
   German, French, Italian, and Romansch.
10 What did Marconi invent in1901?
    The radio.
11 What sort of music did Louis Armstrong play?
    Jazz.
12 What happens at the end of *Romeo and Juliet*?
    Romeo and Juliet kill themselves.
13 What happened in Europe in 1939?
    The Second World War started.
14 Why do birds migrate?
    Because the winter is cold.
15 Which was the first country to have TV?
    Britain.
16 Which language has the most words?
    English.

T 13.2 Listen carefully!

1 Why do you want to go?
2 Who is she?
3 Where's he staying?
4 Why didn't they come?
5 How old was she?
6 Does he play the guitar?
7 Where did you go at the weekend?

T 13.3 Noises in the night

It was about 2 o'clock in the morning, and … suddenly I woke up. I heard a noise. I got out of bed and went slowly downstairs. There was a light on in the living room. I listened carefully. I could hear two men speaking very quietly. 'Burglars!' I thought. 'Two burglars!' Immediately I ran back upstairs and phoned the police. I was really frightened. Fortunately the police arrived quickly. They opened the front door and went into the living room. Then they came upstairs to find me. 'It's all right now, sir,' they explained. 'We turned the television off for you!'

T 13.4 see p102

T 13.5 see p104

T 13.6 Catching a train

Trains from Oxford to Bristol Temple Meads. Monday to Friday.
Here are the departure times from Oxford and arrival times in Bristol.

0816 arriving 0946
0945 arriving 1114
1040 arriving 1208
11…

T 13.7 The information bureau

A = Ann   B = clerk

A Good morning. Can you tell me the times of trains from Bristol back to Oxford, please?
B Afternoon, evening? When do you want to come back?
A About five o'clock this afternoon.
B About five o'clock. Right. Let's have a look. There's a train that leaves at 5.28, then there isn't another one until 6.50.
A And what time do they get in?
B The 5.28 gets into Oxford at 6.54 and the 6.50 gets in at 8.10.
A Thanks a lot.

T 13.8 At the ticket office

A Hello. A return to Bristol, please.
C Day return or period return?
A A day return.
C How do you want to pay?
A Cash, please.
C That's eighteen pounds.
A Here's a twenty-pound note.
C Here's your change and your ticket.
A Thank you. Which platform is it?
C You want platform 1 over there.
A OK, thanks very much. Goodbye.

Unit 14

T 14.1 see p106

T 14.2 see p106

T 14.3 The life of Ryan

Yes, I've lived in a foreign country. In Japan, actually. I lived in Osaka for a year. I enjoyed it very much. I loved the food. And, yes, I have worked for a big company. I worked for Nissan, the car company, that's why I was in Japan. That was two years ago, then I got another job.

Have I stayed in an expensive hotel? No, never – only cheap hotels for me, I'm afraid, but I have flown in a jumbo jet – four or five times, actually. Oh, I've never cooked a meal for a lot of people. I love food but I don't like cooking, sometimes I cook for me and my girlfriend but she likes it better if we go out for a meal! And I've never met a famous person – oh, just a minute, well not met but I've seen … er… I saw a famous politician at the airport once – Oh, who was it? I can't remember his name. Er … I've only seen one Shakespeare play, when I was at school, we saw *Romeo and Juliet*. It was OK. I've driven a tractor though, I had a holiday job on a farm when I was 17. I enjoyed that. Good news – I've never been to hospital. I was born in hospital, of course, but that's different. Bad news – I've never won a competition. I do the lottery every week but I've never, ever won a thing!

T 14.4 A honeymoon in London

M = Marilyn   J = Judy

M We're having a great time!
J Tell me about it! What have you done so far?
M Well, we've been to Buckingham Palace. That was the first thing we did. It's right in the centre of London! We went inside and looked around.
J Have you seen the Houses of Parliament yet?
M Yeah, we have. We've just had a boat ride on the River Thames and we went right past the Houses of Parliament. We saw Big Ben! Then we went on the London Eye. That's the big wheel near Big Ben. That was this morning. This afternoon we're going to take a taxi to Hyde Park and then go shopping in Harrods. Tomorrow morning we're going to see the Crown Jewels in the Tower of London.
J Wow! You're busy! And what about those big red buses? Have you travelled on a double-decker bus yet?
M Oh, yeah we took one when we went to Buckingham Palace. We sat upstairs. You get a great view of the city.
J Tomorrow's your last night. What are you going to do on your last night?
M Well, we're going to the theatre, but we haven't decided what to see yet.
J Oh, you're so lucky! Give my love to Rod!
M Yeah. Bye, Judy. See you soon!

T 14.5 Leaving on a jet plane

My bags are packed, I'm ready to go
I'm standing here outside your door,
I hate to wake you up to say goodbye
But the dawn is breaking,
It's early morn'
The taxi's waiting,
He's blowing his horn.
Already I'm so lonesome
I could die.

So kiss me and smile for me,
Tell me that you'll wait for me,
Hold me like you'll never let me go,
'Cos I'm leaving on a jet plane,
I don't know when I'll be back again.
Oh babe, I hate to go.

There's so many times I've let you down,
So many times I've played around,
I tell you now
They don't mean a thing.
Every place I go, I'll think of you
Every song I sing, I'll sing for you
When I come back
I'll wear your wedding ring.

T 14.6 Flight information

British Airways flight BA 516 to Geneva boarding at gate 4, last call. Flight BA 516 to Geneva, last call. Scandinavian Airlines flight SK 832 to Frankfurt is delayed one hour. Flight SK 832 to Frankfurt, delayed one hour. Air France flight 472 to Amsterdam is now boarding at gate 17. Flight AF 472 to Amsterdam, now boarding, gate 17. Lufthansa flight 309 to Miami is now boarding at gate 32. Flight LH 309 to Miami, now boarding, gate 32. Virgin Airlines flight to New York, flight VS 876 to New York. Please wait in the departure lounge until a further announcement. Thank you. Passengers are reminded to keep their hand luggage with them at all times.

T 14.7 Conversations at the airport

1 A Listen! … BA516 to Geneva. That's our flight.
   B Did the announcement say gate 4 or 14?
   A I couldn't hear. I think it said 4.
   B Look! There it is on the departure board. It *is* gate 4.
   A OK. Come on! Let's go.

2 A Can I have your ticket, please?
   B Yes, of course.
   A Thank you. How many suitcases have you got?
   B Just one.
   A And have you got much hand luggage?
   B Just this bag.
   A That's fine.
   B Oh … can I have a seat next to the window?
   A Yes, that's OK. Here's your boarding pass. Have a nice flight!

3 A Rod! Marilyn! Over here!
   B Hi! Judy! Great to see you!
   A It's great to see you too. You look terrific! Did you have a good honeymoon?
   B Fantastic. Everything was fantastic.
   A Well, you haven't missed anything here. Nothing much has happened at all!

4 A There's my flight. It's time to go.
   B Oh no! It's been a wonderful two weeks. I can't believe it's over.
   A I know. When can we see each other again?
   B Soon, I hope. I'll write every day.
   A I'll phone too. Goodbye.
   B Goodbye. Give my love to your family.

Grammar Reference

Unit 8

8.1 Past Simple

Negative
Negatives in the Past Simple are the same in all persons.

I He/She We You They	didn't	go out see Tom watch TV	last night.

ago

I went to the USA	ten years two weeks a month	ago.

8.2 Time expressions

in	the twentieth century 1924 the 1990s winter/summer the evening/the morning September
on	10 October Christmas Day Saturday Sunday evening
at	seven o'clock weekends night

8.3 Prepositions

What's **on** television this evening?
I'm **on** a mobile phone.
We spoke for an hour **on** the phone.
Some people try to find love **on** the internet.
We didn't laugh **at** his joke.
There was a knock **at** the door.
Today's the third **of** April.

Unit 9

9.1 Count and uncount nouns

Some nouns are countable.
    a book   two books
    an egg   six eggs
Some nouns are uncountable.
    bread   rice
Some nouns are both!
    Do you like ice-cream?
    We'd like three ice-creams, please.

9.2 *would like*

Would is the same in all persons. We use *would like* in offers and requests.

Positive

I You He/She/It We They	'd like	a drink.	'd = would

Yes/No questions

Would	you he/she/it they	like a biscuit?

Short answers

Yes, please.
No, thank you.

9.3 *some* and *any*

We use *some* in positive sentences with uncountable nouns and plural nouns.

There is	some	bread	on the table.
There are		oranges	

We use *some* in questions when we ask for things and offer things.

Can I have	some	coffee, please?	(I know there is some coffee.)
Would you like		grapes?	(I know there are some grapes.)

We use *any* in questions and negative sentences with uncountable nouns and plural nouns.

Is there	any	water?	(I don't know if there is any water.)
Does she have		children?	(I don't know if she has any children.)
I can't see		rice.	
There aren't		people.	

9.4 *How much . . . ?* and *How many . . . ?*

We use *How much . . . ?* with uncount nouns.
    How much rice is there?
    There isn't much rice.
We use *How many . . . ?* with count nouns.
    How many apples are there?
    There aren't many apples.

9.5 Prepositions

I've got a book **by** John Grisham.
Help me **with** my homework.

Unit 10

10.1 Comparative and superlative adjectives

	Adjective	Comparative	Superlative
One-syllable adjectives	old safe big hot	older safer bigger hotter	the oldest the safest the biggest* the hottest*
Adjectives ending in -y	noisy dirty	noisier dirtier	the noisiest the dirtiest
Adjectives with two or more syllables	boring beautiful	**more** boring **more** beautiful	the **most** boring the **most** beautiful
Irregular adjectives	good bad far	**better** **worse** **further**	the **best** the **worst** the **furthest**

* Adjectives which end in one vowel and one consonant double the consonant.

> You're **older than** me.
> New York is **dirtier than** Paris.
> Prague is one of **the most beautiful** cities in Europe.

10.2 *have got* and *have*

Have got means the same as *have* to talk about possession, but the form is very different. We often use *have got* in spoken English.

have got

Positive

I You We They	have	got	a cat. a garden.
He She It	has		

Negative

I You We They	haven't	got	a dog. a garage.
He She It	hasn't		

Questions

Have	I you we they	got	any money? a sister?
Has	he she it		

How many children **have they got**?

Short answers
Yes, I have./No, I haven't.
Yes, she has./No, she hasn't.

have

Positive

I You We They	have		a cat. a garden.
He She It	has		

Negative

I You We They	don't	have	a dog. a garage.
He She It	doesn't		

Questions

Do	I you we they	have	any money? a sister?
Does	he she it		

How many children **do they have**?

Short answers
Yes, I do./No, I don't.
Yes, she does./No, she doesn't.

The past of both *have* and *have got* is *had*.

10.3 Prepositions

The country is quieter **than** the city.
The house is 50 metres **from** the sea.
Everest is the highest mountain **in** the world.
He spends his time **on** the banks of the river.
She came **out of** the garage.
He drove **along** the road.
They ran **over** the bridge.
I walked **past** the pub.
He walked **up** the hill.
He ran **down** the hill.
The boat went **across** the river.
The cat ran **through** the hedge.
He jumped **into** the lake.

Unit 11

11.1 Present Continuous

1 The Present Continuous describes an activity happening now.
   She**'s wearing** jeans.
   I**'m studying** English.

2 It also describes an activity in the near future.
   I**'m playing** tennis this afternoon.
   Jane**'s seeing** her boyfriend tonight.

Positive and Negative

I	am		
He She It	is	(not) going	outside.
We You They	are		

Question

	am	I	
Where	is	he/she/it	going?
	are	we you they	

Yes/No **questions**	**Short answers**
Are you having a good time?	Yes, we are.
Is my English getting better?	Yes, it is.
Are they having a party?	No, they aren't.

Spelling of verb + -ing

1 Most verbs just add -ing.
wear	wea**ring**
go	go**ing**
cook	cook**ing**
hold	hold**ing**

2 If the infinitive ends in -e, drop the -e.
write	writ**ing**
smile	smil**ing**
take	tak**ing**

3 When a one-syllable verb has one vowel and ends in a consonant, double the consonant.
sit	sit**t**ing
get	get**t**ing
run	run**n**ing

11.2 Present Simple and Present Continuous

1 The Present Simple describes things that are always true, or true for a long time.
   I **come** from Switzerland.
   He **works** in a bank.

2 The Present Continuous describes activities happening now, and temporary activities.
   Why **are you wearing** a suit? You usually wear jeans.

11.3 *Whose* + possessive pronouns

Whose ... ? asks about possession.

Subject	Object	Adjective	Pronoun
I	me	my	mine
You	you	your	yours
He	him	his	his
She	her	her	hers
We	us	our	ours
They	them	their	theirs

Whose is this book? Whose book is this? Whose is it?	It's	mine. yours. hers. his. ours. theirs.

11.4 Prepositions

I read **in** bed.
We've got this jumper **in** red.
He's talking **to** Mandy.
There's a girl **with** fair hair.
I'm looking **for** a jumper.
I always pay **by** credit card.

Unit 12

12.1 *going to*

1 *Going to* expresses a person's plans and intentions.
   She's **going to** be a ballet dancer when she grows up.
   We're **going to** stay in a villa in France this summer.

2 Often there is no difference between *going to* and the Present Continuous to refer to a future intention.
   I'**m seeing** Peter tonight.
   I'**m going to see** Peter tonight.

3 We also use *going to* when we can see now that something is sure to happen in the future.
   Careful! That glass is **going to** fall!

Positive and negative

I	am		
He/She/It	is	(not) going to	have a break.
We You They	are		stay at home.

Question

	am	I		
When	is	he/she/it	going to	have a break?
	are	we you they		stay at home?

With the verbs *to go* and *to come*, we usually use the Present Continuous for future plans.
   We'**re going** to Paris next week.
   Joe and Tim **are coming** for lunch tomorrow.

12.2 Infinitive of purpose

The infinitive can express why a person does something.
   I'm saving my money **to buy** a CD player.
   (= because I want to buy a CD player)

   We're going to Paris **to have** a holiday.
   (= because we want to have a holiday)

   NOT
   I'm saving my money ~~for to buy~~ a CD player.
   I'm saving my money ~~for buy~~ a CD player.

12.3 Prepositions

I'm going to Florida **in** a year's time.
He's interested **in** flying.
She's good **at** singing.
She was afraid **of** cars.
What's the weather **like**?
What's **on** TV tonight?
There's a film **on** Channel 4.
What's **on at** the cinema?

Unit 13

13.1 Question forms

When did Columbus discover America?
Where are the Andes?
Who did she marry?
Who was Mother Teresa?
How do you get to school?
What do you have for breakfast?
What happens at the end of the story?
Why do you want to learn English?

How many people are there in the class?
How much does she earn?
How far is it to the centre?
What sort of car do you have?
Which newspaper do you read?

13.2 Adjectives and adverbs

Adjectives describe nouns.
   a **big** dog
   a **careful** driver

Adverbs describe verbs.
   She ran **quickly**.
   He drives too **fast**.

To form regular adverbs, add *-ly* to the adjective.
Words ending in *-y* change to *-ily*.

Adjective	Adverb
quick	quickly
bad	badly
careful	carefully
immediate	immediately
easy	easily

Some adverbs are irregular.

Adjective	Adverb
good	well
hard	hard
early	early
fast	fast

13.3 Prepositions

What's the story **about**?
What happens **at** the end of the story?
The train leaves **from** platform 9.

Unit 14

14.1 Present Perfect

1 The Present Perfect refers to an action that happened some time before now.
   She**'s travelled** to most parts of the world.
   Have you ever **been** in a car accident?

2 If we want to say *when* these actions happened, we must use the Past Simple.
   She **went** to Russia two years ago.
   I **was** in a crash when I was 10.

3 Notice the time expressions used with the Past Simple.

I left	last night. yesterday. in 1990. at three o'clock. on Monday.

Positive and negative

I You We They	have	(not) been	to the States.
He She It	has		

I've been = I have been
You've been = You have been
We've been = We have been
They've been = They have been

He's been = He has been
She's been = She has been
It's been = It has been

Question

Where	have	I you we they	been?
	has	she he it	

Yes/No **questions**
Have you been to Russia?

Short answers
Yes, I have.
No, I haven't.

ever and never

We use *ever* in questions and *never* in negative sentences.
   Have you **ever** been to Russia?
   I've **never** been to Russia.

14.2 yet and just

We use *just* in positive sentences. We use *yet* in negative sentences and questions.
   Have you done your homework **yet**?
   I haven't done it **yet** (but I'm going to).
   I have **just** done it (a short time before now).

14.3 been and gone

She's **gone** to Portugal (and she's there now).
She's **been** to Portugal (sometime in her life, but now she has returned).

14.4 Prepositions

She works **for** a big company.
Hamlet is a play **by** Shakespeare.
Brad and Marilyn are **on** honeymoon
Wait **for** me!

Word list

Here is a list of most of the new words in the units of New Headway Elementary.

adj = adjective
adv = adverb
conj = conjunction
opp = opposite
pl = plural
prep = preposition
pron = pronoun
pp = past participle
n = noun
v = verb
infml = informal
US = American English

Unit 8

(3 years) ago *adv* /ə'gəʊ/
(coffee) break *n* /breɪk/
arthritis *n* /ɑ:θ'raɪtɪs/
aspirin *n* /'æsprɪn/
astronaut *n* /'æstrənɔ:t/
banana *n* /bə'nɑ:nə/
beach *n* /bi:tʃ/
bestselling *adj* /'best'selɪŋ/
blue *adj* /blu:/
bottle *n* /'bɒtl/
boy *n* /bɔɪ/
chat *v* /tʃæt/
chatline *n* /'tʃætlaɪn/
chicken *n* /'tʃɪkɪn/
clock *n* /klɒk/
cloth *n* /klɒθ/
company *n* /'kʌmpəni/
couple *n pl* /'kʌpl/
date *n* /deɪt/
delicious *adj* /dɪ'lɪʃəs/
drug *n* /drʌg/
e-mail *n* /'i:meɪl/
exam *n* /ɪg'zæm/
face *n* /feɪs/
face to face /'feɪs tə 'feɪs/
fashionable *adj* /'fæʃnəbl/
fax *n* /fæks/
fisherman *n* /'fɪʃəmən/
funny *adj* /'fʌni/
get engaged *v* /ˌget ɪn'geɪdʒd/
get married *v* /ˌget 'mærɪd/
go to a party *v* /ˌgəʊ tu: ə 'pɑ:ti/
good luck! /ˌgʊd 'lʌk/
green *adj* /gri:n/
in a hurry /ˌɪn ə 'hʌri/
incredible *adj* /ɪn'kredəbl/
internet *n* /'ɪntənet/
invention *n* /ɪn'venʃn/
jeans *n pl* /dʒi:nz/
joke *n* /dʒəʊk/
leg *n* /leg/
mobile phone *n* /'məʊbaɪl 'fəʊn/
moon *n* /mu:n/
mouth *n* /maʊθ/
nervous *adj* /'nɜ:vəs/
nowadays *adv* /'naʊədeɪz/
painkiller *n* /'peɪnkɪlə/
philosopher *n* /fɪ'lɒsəfə/
phone call *n* /'fəʊn ˌkɔ:l/
produce *v* /prə'dju:s/
public holiday *n* /'pʌblɪk 'hɒlədeɪ/
recipe *n* /'resəpi/
record (for music) *n* /'rekɔ:d/
ride *v* /raɪd/
rose *n* /rəʊz/
send *v* /send/

take *v* /teɪk/
term *n* /tɜ:m/
them *pron* /ðem/
throw *v* /θrəʊ/
transmit *v* /trænz'mɪt/
trousers *n pl* /'traʊzəz/
true *adj* /tru:/
true love *n* /ˌtru: 'lʌv/
vacuum cleaner *n*
    /'vækju:m ˌkli:nə/
watch *v* /wɒtʃ/
way *n* /weɪ/
women *n pl* /'wɪmɪn/
workmen *n pl*
    /'wɜ:kmen/, /'wɜ:kmən/
workroom *n* /'wɜ:krʊm/
worried *adj* /'wʌrid/

Unit 9

a bit *n* /ə ˈbɪt/
all sorts *n pl* /ˈɔːl ˈsɔːts/
anybody *pron* /ˈenibɒdi/
anyway *adv* /ˈeniweɪ/
apple juice *n* /ˈæpl ˌdʒuːs/
away from *adv* /əˈweɪ frəm/
bacon *n* /ˈbeɪkən/
bag *n* /bæg/
bar of chocolate *n*
    /ˈbɑː(r) əv ˈtʃɒklət/
beer *n* /bɪə/
birthday *n* /ˈbɜːθdeɪ/
biscuit *n* /ˈbɪskɪt/
black (coffee) *adj* /blæk/
borrow *v* /ˈbɒrəʊ/
bottle *n* /ˈbɒtəl/
bread *n* /bred/
carrot *n* /ˈkærət/
central *adj* /ˈsentrəl/
cheese *n* /tʃiːz/
China *n* /ˈtʃaɪnə/
Chinese *adj* /tʃaɪˈniːz/
chopsticks *n pl* /ˈtʃɒpstɪks/
cigarette *n* /sɪgəˈret/
control *v* /kənˈtrəʊl/
course (of a meal) *n* /kɔːs/
curry *n* /ˈkʌri/
dangerous *adj* /ˈdeɪndʒərəs/
depend *v* /dɪˈpend/
dessert *n* /dɪˈzɜːt/
disgusting *adj* /dɪsˈgʌstɪŋ/
easily *adv* /ˈiːzəli/
egg *n* /eg/
either *adv* /ˈaɪðə/
environment *n* /ɪnˈvaɪrənmənt/
especially /ɪˈspeʃəli/
farm *v* /fɑːm/
finger *n* /ˈfɪŋgə/
fish *n* /fɪʃ/
fizzy water *n* /ˈfɪzi ˈwɔːtə/
for example /ˌfɔː(r) ɪgˈzɑːmpl/
foreign *adj* /ˈfɒrɪn/
fruit *n* /fruːt/
full *adj* /fʊl/
glad *adj* /glæd/
ham *n* /hæm/
herring *n* /ˈherɪŋ/
history *n* /ˈhɪstəri/
horrible *adj* /ˈhɒrəbl/
human *adj* /ˈhjuːmən/
hungry *adj* /ˈhʌŋgri/
land *n* /lænd/
main (meal) *adj* /meɪn/
meal *n* /miːl/
meat *n* /miːt/
milk *n* /mɪlk/
money *n* /ˈmʌni/
mushroom *n* /ˈmʌʃrʊm/
noodles *n pl* /ˈnuːdlz/
north *n* /nɔːθ/
part (of the world) *n* /pɑːt/
pass (= give) *v* /pɑːs/
pasta *n* /ˈpæstə/

pea *n* /piː/
petrol *n* /ˈpetrəl/
pick up *v* /ˌpɪk ˈʌp/
pocket *n* /ˈpɒkɪt/
poor *adj* /pʊə/, /pɔː/
possible *adj* /ˈpɒsəbl/
potatoes *n pl* /pəˈteɪtəʊz/
rice *n* /raɪs/
right now *adv* /ˌraɪt ˈnaʊ/
salt *n* /sɔːlt/, /sɒlt/
sardine *n* /sɑːˈdiːn/
sauce *n* /sɔːs/
sausages *n pl* /ˈsɒsɪdʒɪz/
shopping list *n* /ˈʃɒpɪŋ ˌlɪst/
south *n* /saʊθ/
still water *n* /ˈstɪl ˈwɔːtə/
strawberry *n* /ˈstrɔːbəri/
sugar *n* /ˈʃʊgə/
table *n* /ˈteɪbl/
terrible *adj* /ˈterəbl/
toast *n* /təʊst/
together *adv* /təˈgeðə/
tomato *n* /təˈmɑːtəʊ/
transport *v* /trænˈspɔːt/
typical *adj* /ˈtɪpɪkl/
vegetable *n* /ˈvedʒtəbl/
washing-up *n* /ˌwɒʃɪŋ ˈʌp/
wonderful *adj* /ˈwʌndəfʊl/
yoghurt *n* /ˈjɒgət/

Unit 10

art *n* /ɑːt/
blues (music) *n pl* /bluːz/
bridge *n* /brɪdʒ/
building *n* /ˈbɪldɪŋ/
busy *adj* /ˈbɪzi/
car park *n* /ˈkɑː ˌpɑːk/
carnival *n* /ˈkɑːnɪvl/
castle *n* /ˈkɑːsl/
cathedral *n* /kəˈθiːdrəl/
church *n* /tʃɜːtʃ/
clean *adj* /kliːn/
cosmopolitan *adj*
    /ˌkɒzməˈpɒlɪtən/
cottage *n* /ˈkɒtɪdʒ/
country (not the city) *n* /ˈkʌntri/
cousin *n* /ˈkʌzən/
cultural centre *n*
    /ˈkʌltʃərəl ˌsentə/
dangerous *adj* /ˈdeɪndʒərəs/
dirty *adj* /ˈdɜːti/
empire *n* /ˈempaɪə/
expensive *adj* /ɪkˈspensɪv/
factory *n* /ˈfæktri/
field *n* /fiːld/
found (a university) *v* /faʊnd/
garage *n* /ˈgærɪdʒ/, /ˈgærɑːʒ/
garden *n* /ˈgɑːdn/
gateway *n* /ˈgeɪtweɪ/
group *n* /gruːp/
hedge *n* /hedʒ/
hill *n* /hɪl/
hotel *n* /həʊˈtel/
hymn *n* /hɪm/
immigrants *n pl* /ˈɪmɪgrənts/
intelligent *adj* /ɪnˈtelɪdʒənt/
library *n* /ˈlaɪbrəri/
mixture *n* /ˈmɪkstʃə/
mountain *n* /ˈmaʊntɪn/
museum *n* /mjuːˈzɪəm/
night club *n* /ˈnaɪt ˌklʌb/
noisy *adj* /ˈnɔɪzi/
orchestra *n* /ˈɔːkɪstrə/
passenger *n* /ˈpæsɪndʒə/
popular *adj* /ˈpɒpjʊlə/
port *n* /pɔːt/
pretty *adj* /ˈprɪti/
quiet *adj* /ˈkwaɪət/
restaurant *n* /ˈrestrɒnt/
river bank *n* /ˈrɪvə ˌbæŋk/
rock group *n* /ˈrɒk ˌgruːp/
safe *adj* /seɪf/
ship *n* /ʃɪp/
small *adj* /smɔːl/
song *n* /sɒŋ/
spices *n pl* /ˈspaɪsɪz/
stand *v* /stænd/
street *n* /striːt/
tall *adj* /tɔːl/

the Underground *n*
    /ði ˈʌndəgraʊnd/
top ten (music) *n* /ˌtɒp ˈten/
travel *n* /ˈtrævl/
unfriendly *adj* /ʌnˈfrendli/
village *n* /ˈvɪlɪdʒ/
wood *n* /wʊd/

Unit 11

baby *n* /'beɪbi/
baseball cap *n* /'beɪsbɔːl ˌkæp/
beautiful *adj* /'bjuːtɪfl/
bloom *v* /bluːm/
boot *n* /buːt/
bright *adj* /braɪt/
changing rooms *n pl*
    /'tʃeɪndʒɪŋ ˌruːmz/
chewing gum *n* /'tʃuːɪŋ ˌgʌm/
choose *v* /tʃuːz/
cigar *n* /sɪ'gɑː/
cloud *n* /klaʊd/
coat *n* /kəʊt/
credit card *n* /'kredɪt ˌkɑːd/
cry *v* /kraɪ/
dark *adj* /dɑːk/
dress *n* /dres/
eat *v* /iːt/
fair (hair) *adj* /feə/
fresh *adj* /freʃ/
good-looking *adj* /ˌgʊd'lʊkɪŋ/
grey *adj* /greɪ/
guest *n* /gest/
hair *n* /heə/
half *n* /hɑːf/
handsome *adj* /'hænsəm/
hat *n* /hæt/
hill *n* /hɪl/
jacket *n* /'dʒækɪt/
jumper *n* /'dʒʌmpə/
laugh *v* /lɑːf/
long *adj* /lɒŋ/
musician *n* /mjuː'zɪʃn/
pay *v* /peɪ/
pram *n* /præm/
rainbow *n* /'reɪnbəʊ/
roller skates *n pl* /'rəʊlə ˌskeɪts/
run *v* /rʌn/
shake *v* /ʃeɪk/
shiny *adj* /'ʃaɪni/
shirt *n* /ʃɜːt/
shoe *n* /ʃuː/
short *adj* /ʃɔːt/
shorts *n pl* /ʃɔːts/
silly *adj* /'sɪli/
size *n* /saɪz/
skateboard *n* /'skeɪtbɔːd/
skirt *n* /skɜːt/
sky *n* /skaɪ/
smile *v* /smaɪl/
smoke *v* /sməʊk/
sports car *n* /'spɔːts ˌkɑː/
starry *adj* /'stɑːri/
suit *n* /suːt/
sunglasses *n pl* /'sʌnglɑːsɪz/
T-shirt *n* /'tiːˌʃɜːt/
talk *v* /tɔːk/
trainers *n pl* /'treɪnəz/
try on *v* /ˌtraɪ 'ɒn/
umbrella *n* /ʌm'brelə/
whose? *pron* /huːz/

Unit 12

accident *n* /'æksɪdənt/
adventure *n* /əd'ventʃə/
amazed *adj* /ə'meɪzd/
blouse *n* /blaʊz/
championship *n* /'tʃæmpiənʃɪp/
cloudy *adj* /'klaʊdi/
coast *n* /kəʊst/
cool *adj* /kuːl/
corner *n* /'kɔːnə/
degrees *n pl* /dɪ'griːz/
driving school *n* /'draɪvɪŋ ˌskuːl/
dry *adj* /draɪ/
excitement *n* /ɪk'saɪtmənt/
feel sick *v* /ˌfiːl 'sɪk/
float *v* /fləʊt/
foggy *adj* /'fɒgi/
forever *adv* /fɔː'r'evə/
forget *v* /fə'get/
fresh air *n* /ˌfreʃ 'eə/
full-time *adj* /ˌfʊl'taɪm/
garden shed *n* /ˌgɑːdn 'ʃed/
golf *n* /gɒlf/
grow up *v* /ˌgrəʊ 'ʌp/
lion *n* /'laɪən/
motor racing *n* /'məʊtə ˌreɪsɪŋ/
nervous *adj* /'nɜːvəs/
parachute *n* /'pærəʃuːt/
pyramid *n* /'pɪrəmɪd/
race *v* /reɪs/
racing circuit *n* /'reɪsɪŋ ˌsɜːkɪt/
racing driver *n* /'reɪsɪŋ ˌdraɪvə/
record *n* /'rekɔːd/
retire *v* /rɪ'taɪə/
safe *adj* /seɪf/
sky diving *n* /'skaɪ ˌdaɪvɪŋ/
sneeze *v* /sniːz/
star (TV) *n* /stɑː/
sunbathe *v* /'sʌnbeɪð/
swimming costume *n*
    /'swɪmɪŋ ˌkɒstjuːm/
top marks *n pl* /'tɒp 'mɑːks/
trouble *n* /'trʌbl/
tulip *n* /'tjuːlɪp/
view *n* /vjuː/
weather *n* /'weθə/
windsurfing *n* /'wɪndsɜːfɪŋ/
windy *adj* /'wɪndi/

Unit 13

annoyed *adj* /ə'nɔɪd/
arrive *v* /ə'raɪv/
badly *adv* /'bædli/
behave *v* /bɪ'heɪv/
behaviour *n* /bɪ'heɪvɪə/
burglar *n* /'bɜːglə/
carefully *adv* /'keəfəli/
change (= money) *n* /tʃeɪndʒ/
depart *v* /dɪ'paːt/
elephant *n* /'elɪfənt/
explain *v* /ɪk'spleɪn/
fast *adv* /faːst/
fluently *adv* /'fluːəntli/
fortunately *adv* /'fɔːtʃənətli/
generation *n* /ˌdʒenə'reɪʃn/
gold medal *n* /'gəʊld 'medl/
grass *n* /graːs/
guitar *n* /gɪ'tɒ/
leather *n* /'leðə/
marathon *n* /'mærəθən/
migrate *v* /maɪ'greɪt/
moon *n* /muːn/
pin *v* /pɪn/
platform *n* /'plætfɔːm/
please *v* /pliːz/
quietly *adv* /'kwaɪətli/
return ticket *n* /rɪ'tɜːn 'tɪkɪt/
ridiculous *adj* /rɪ'dɪkjələs/
rude *adj* /ruːd/
sheep *n* /ʃiːp/
shout *v* /ʃaʊt/
slowly *adv* /'sləʊli/
station *n* /'steɪʃn/
support (a team) *v* /sə'pɔːt/
tell a lie *v* /ˌtel ə 'laɪ/
timetable *n* /'taɪmteɪbl/
typical *adj* /'tɪpɪkl/
untidy *adj* /ʌn'taɪdi/
weigh *v* /weɪ/
well-behaved *adj* /ˌwel bɪ'heɪvd/
whistle *v* /'wɪsl/
wolf *n* /wʊlf/
worrying *adj* /'wʌrɪɪŋ/

Unit 14

abroad *adv* /ə'brɔːd/
airport *n* /'eəpɔːt/
ambulance driver *n*
    /'æmbjələns ˌdraɪvə/
announcement *n* /ə'naʊnsmənt/
arrival hall *n* /ə'raɪvl ˌhɔːl/
board *v* /bɔːd/
boarding pass *n* /'bɔːdɪŋ ˌpaːs/
boat ride *n* /'bəʊt ˌraɪd/
business class *n* /'bɪznəs ˌklaːs/
call *n* /kɔːl/
certificate *n* /sə'tɪfɪkət/
check in *v* /ˌtʃek 'ɪn/
check-in desk *n* /'tʃek ɪn ˌdesk/
competition *n* /ˌkɒmpə'tɪʃn/
crown *n* /kraʊn/
dawn *n* /dɔːn/
delay *v* /dɪ'leɪ/
delayed *pp* /dɪ'leɪd/
departures board *n*
    /dɪ'paːtʃəz ˌbɔːd/
departure lounge *n*
    /dɪ'paːtʃə ˌlaʊndʒ/
double-decker bus *n*
    /ˌdʌbl ˌdekə 'bʌs/
dressmaker *n* /'dresmeɪkə/
engineer *n* /ˌendʒɪ'nɪə/
flag *n* /flæg/
flight *n* /flaɪt/
gate (in an airport) *n* /geɪt/
give up (= stop) *v* /ˌgɪv 'ʌp/
grandson *n* /'grænˌsʌn/
Greece *n* /griːs/
heart attack *n* /'haːt əˌtæk/
honeymoon *n* /'hʌnimuːn/
horn (on a car) *n* /hɔːn/
Hungary *n* /'hʌŋgəri/
jewels *n pl* /'dʒuːəlz/
jumbo jet *n* /'dʒʌmbəʊ 'dʒet/
jump *v* /dʒʌmp/
last call *n* /ˌlaːst 'kɔːl/
let (sb) down (= disappoint) *v*
    /ˌlet 'daʊn/
lottery *n* /'lɒtəri/
loud *adj* /laʊd/
luggage *n* /'lʌgɪdʒ/
lung cancer *n* /'lʌŋ ˌkænsə/
marmalade *n* /'maːməleɪd/
millionaire *n* /ˌmɪljə'neə/
miss *v* /mɪs/
niece *n* /niːs/
now boarding /ˌnaʊ 'bɔːdɪŋ/
pack (a bag) *v* /pæk/
passenger *n* /'pæsɪndʒə/
passport control
    /'paːspɔːt kən'trəʊl/
pipe (to smoke) *n* /paɪp/
pneumonia *n* /njuː'məʊnɪə/
remind *v* /rɪ'maɪnd/
rheumatic fever *n*
    /ruː'mætɪk 'fiːvə/

seat *n* /siːt/
secretary *n* /'sekrətri/
serious *adj* /'sɪərɪəs/
suitcase *n* /'suːtkeɪs/
tractor *n* /'træktə/
trolley *n* /'trɒli/

Appendix 1

Base form	Past Simple	Past Participle
be	was/were	been
become	became	become
begin	began	begun
break	broke	broken
bring	brought	brought
build	built	built
buy	bought	bought
can	could	been able
catch	caught	caught
choose	chose	chosen
come	came	come
cost	cost	cost
cut	cut	cut
do	did	done
drink	drank	drunk
drive	drove	driven
eat	ate	eaten
fall	fell	fallen
feel	felt	felt
fight	fought	fought
find	found	found
fly	flew	flown
forget	forgot	forgotten
get	got	got
give	gave	given
go	went	gone/been
grow	grew	grown
have	had	had
hear	heard	heard
hit	hit	hit
keep	kept	kept
know	knew	known
learn	learnt/learned	learnt/learned
leave	left	left
lose	lost	lost
make	made	made
meet	met	met
pay	paid	paid
put	put	put
read /riːd/	read /red/	read /red/
ride	rode	ridden
run	ran	run
say	said	said
see	saw	seen
sell	sold	sold
send	sent	sent
shut	shut	shut
sing	sang	sung
sit	sat	sat
sleep	slept	slept
speak	spoke	spoken
spend	spent	spent
stand	stood	stood
steal	stole	stolen
swim	swam	swum
take	took	taken
tell	told	told
think	thought	thought
understand	understood	understood
wake	woke	woken
wear	wore	worn
win	won	won
write	wrote	written

Appendix 2

Verb + -ing	
like	
love	swimming
enjoy	
hate	cooking
finish	
stop	

Verb + to + infinitive	
choose	
decide	
forget	
promise	to go
need	
help	
hope	
try	to work
want	
would like	
would love	

Verb + -ing or to + infinitive	
begin	raining/to rain
start	

Modal auxiliary verbs	
can	
could	go
shall	
will	arrive
would	

Phonetic symbols

Consonants

1	/p/	as in	**pen**	/pen/
2	/b/	as in	**big**	/bɪg/
3	/t/	as in	**tea**	/tiː/
4	/d/	as in	**do**	/duː/
5	/k/	as in	**cat**	/kæt/
6	/g/	as in	**go**	/gəʊ/
7	/f/	as in	**four**	/fɔː/
8	/v/	as in	**very**	/ˈveri/
9	/s/	as in	**son**	/sʌn/
10	/z/	as in	**zoo**	/zuː/
11	/l/	as in	**live**	/lɪv/
12	/m/	as in	**my**	/maɪ/
13	/n/	as in	**near**	/nɪə/
14	/h/	as in	**happy**	/ˈhæpi/
15	/r/	as in	**red**	/red/
16	/j/	as in	**yes**	/jes/
17	/w/	as in	**want**	/wɒnt/
18	/θ/	as in	**thanks**	/θæŋks/
19	/ð/	as in	**the**	/ðə/
20	/ʃ/	as in	**she**	/ʃiː/
21	/ʒ/	as in	**television**	/ˈtelɪvɪʒn/
22	/tʃ/	as in	**child**	/tʃaɪld/
23	/dʒ/	as in	**German**	/ˈdʒɜːmən/
24	/ŋ/	as in	**English**	/ˈɪŋglɪʃ/

Vowels

25	/iː/	as in	**see**	/siː/
26	/ɪ/	as in	**his**	/hɪz/
27	/i/	as in	**twenty**	/ˈtwenti/
28	/e/	as in	**ten**	/ten/
29	/æ/	as in	**stamp**	/stæmp/
30	/ɑː/	as in	**father**	/ˈfɑːðə/
31	/ɒ/	as in	**hot**	/hɒt/
32	/ɔː/	as in	**morning**	/ˈmɔːnɪŋ/
33	/ʊ/	as in	**football**	/ˈfʊtbɔːl/
34	/uː/	as in	**you**	/juː/
35	/ʌ/	as in	**sun**	/sʌn/
36	/ɜː/	as in	**learn**	/lɜːn/
37	/ə/	as in	**letter**	/ˈletə/

Diphthongs (two vowels together)

38	/eɪ/	as in	**name**	/neɪm/
39	/əʊ/	as in	**no**	/nəʊ/
40	/aɪ/	as in	**my**	/maɪ/
41	/aʊ/	as in	**how**	/haʊ/
42	/ɔɪ/	as in	**boy**	/bɔɪ/
43	/ɪə/	as in	**hear**	/hɪə/
44	/eə/	as in	**where**	/weə/
45	/ʊə/	as in	**tour**	/tʊə/

OXFORD
UNIVERSITY PRESS

Great Clarendon Street, Oxford OX2 6DP

Oxford University Press is a department of the University of Oxford.

It furthers the University's objective of excellence in research, scholarship, and education by publishing worldwide in

Oxford New York

Auckland Bangkok Buenos Aires Cape Town Chennai
Dar es Salaam Delhi Hong Kong Istanbul Karachi
Kolkata Kuala Lumpur Madrid Melbourne
Mexico City Mumbai Nairobi São Paulo
Shanghai Taipei Tokyo Toronto

Oxford and Oxford English are registered trade marks of Oxford University Press in the UK and in certain other countries

© Oxford University Press 2000

The moral rights of the author have been asserted

Database right Oxford University Press (maker)

First published 2000
Third impression 2003

ISBN 0 19 436677 4 Complete Edition
ISBN 0 19 437877 2 Student's Book A
ISBN 0 19 437878 0 Student's Book B

Printed in China

Acknowledgements

The authors and publisher are grateful to those who have given permission to reproduce the following extracts and adaptations of copyright material:
p24 'It's a job for nine men, but someone's got to do it' by Rebecca Fowler. *The Mail Night and Day Magazine* 3 May 1998. © *The Mail on Sunday*.
p40 'The jet settler' by Andy Lines. *The Mirror, Cover Magazine* March 1999. © Mirror Group Newspapers.
p48 'Refugee's daughter hailed as new Picasso' by Nigel Reynolds. *The Daily Telegraph* 12 March 1996. © Telegraph Group Ltd.
p48 'Shy 10-year-old piano prodigy' by David Ward. *The Guardian* 23 September 1997. © *The Guardian*.
p87 'What a wonderful world'. Words and Music by George David Weiss and George Douglas © 1967 Range Road Music, Inc., Quartet Music, Inc. and Abilene Music, Inc., USA. – Copyright Renewed – All Rights

Reserved. 50% Lyric reproduction by kind permission of Carlin Music Corporation, 50% by kind permission of Memory Lane Music Limited.
p102 'The Story-Teller' from Tooth and Claw (Oxford Bookworms Series) by Rosemary Border.
p110 'Discover the secrets of a long life' by Katy Macdonald. *The Daily Mail* 2 November 1993. © *The Daily Mail*.
p112 'Leaving on a jet plane' by John Denver © 1967, Cherry Lane Music Limited, c/o Harmony Music Limited, 11 Uxbridge Street, London W8 7TQ.

Every endeavour has been made to identify the sources of all material used. The publisher apologises for any omissions.

Illustrations by:
Kathy Baxendale pp17, 96; Rowie Christopher pp45, 86–87, 98–99; Martin Cottam pp103, 104; Neil Gower pp43, 81; Jane Hadfield p66; John Holder pp102–3, 104; Sarah Jones pp11, 65; Ian Kellas pp31, 32, 44, 69, 76, 84–5, 92, 97, 100; Andy Parker p84; Pierre Paul Pariseau pp96–7; Debbie Ryder p80; Colin Salmon p40; Harry Venning pp6, 16, 34, 39, 62, 77, 81, 85, 88, 98, 99, 101

The publishers would like to thank the following for their kind permission to reproduce photographs:
AKG Photos pp47 (Mozart), 62 (Levi Strauss), 79 (Eric Lessing/Vienna Operahouse); **Associated Press** pp42 (Susan Sterner/beach), 59 (Big Ben), 74; **Barnabys Picture Library** pp20 (doctor), 26 (nurse), 32 (autumn), 108 (Stuart D Hall/Brad & Marilyn); **Bayer** p62 (Hoffman & Aspirin bottle); **John Birdsill Photography** pp12, 51 (black woman on phone), 82 (Nadia & Rudi), 83 (Flora & Toni); **Catherine Blackie** p110 (Tommy young, Joyce young and old); **Anthony Blake Photo Library** pp26 (John Sims/barman), 71 (John Sims/bananas), 72 (Sian Irving/pasta, Andrew Sydenham/chocolate cakes, Gerrit Buntrock/bacon & eggs); **Bridgeman Art Library** pp56 (The Hall of Representatives/The Signing of the Constitution of the United States in 1787, 1940 by Howard Chandler Christy), 57 (Pennsylvania Academy of Fine Arts, Philadelphia/George Washington at Princeton by Charles Willson Peale 1741–1827), 79 (Coram Foundation/Handel's Messiah); **Camera Press** pp55 (Mark Stewart/ flowers), 56 (M Thatcher & family, Jon Blau/M Thatcher at conference), 61 (cars); **Collections** pp26 (Brian Shuel/shopkeeper, Nick Oakes/architect), 110 (old Tommy), 111 (Anthea Sieveking/Alice old); **Corbis Images** pp47 (Einstein), 53 (cotton picking), 62 (JL Baird); **Corbis Sygma** pp26 (Mathiew/Journalist), 55 (R Ellis/Clinton & Blair), 57 (M Polak/M Thatcher resignation), 82 (Ruth, Cathy & Jane); **Zoe Dominic** p47 (Nureyev); **European Commission** p26 (interpreter); **Format Photographers** pp11 (Joanne O'Brien/Leo), 83 (Ulrike Preuss/Becca); **Greg Evans International** pp42 (Greg Balfour Evans/Alise), 58 (Greg Balfour Evans/Easter Eggs), 112 (Greg Balfour Evans/plane; **Food Features** p72 (Indian curry); **Getty One Stone** pp7 (John Riley/Max & Lisa), 16–17 (Joseph Pobereskin/Central Park), 25 (David Tomlinson), 32 (Manuela, Chad Ehlers/beach), 33 (Bruce Ayres/Toshi, cherry blossom, Rich Iwasaki/ maple trees), 42 (Dennis McColeman/Toronto), 55 (P Crowther & S Carter/Euro Symbol), 58 (Bob Thomas/ wedding), 58 (Bruce Ayres/Thanksgiving, James Randklev/Christmas tree), p59 (Andrew Olney/girl & cake), 64 (Phil Schofield/fisherman, Martin Rogers/ man & laptop, Walter Hodges/girl on computer, Michelangelo Gratton/girl on beach), 64–5 (Mark Andrew/message in bottle), 71 (Wayne astep/Shammar tribe eating, Yann Lavma/China woman & child, David

Baird/strawberry crates), 72 (Martin Barraud/Sally), 73 (Timothy Shonnard), 79 (ferry), 83 (Ian O'Leary/businessman), 86–7 (baby), 93 (Suzanne & Nick Geary/tulips), 93 (safari, Donald Nausbaum/Copacabana Beach, John Lamb/Red Square), 108 (Paul Figura/Ryan); **Sue Glass** p95 (Sue Glass racing & portrait); **The Guardian** p48–9 (Don McPhee/Lukas Vondracek); **Robert Harding Picture Library** pp8 (P Bouchon/Maria), 26 (pilot, Ken Gilham/postman), 32 (Norma Joseph/Al Wheeler), 42 (J Lightfoot/Lisbon, Int Stock/Ray & Elsie), 51 (teenager on phone), 54 (Bob Jacobson/Simon), 59 (Mark Mawson/pumpkin), 72 (Rex Rouchon/Lucy), 76 (Norma Joseph/Plaza), 83 (Tony Demi/Angela, David Hughes/Juan), 93 (pyramids, Taj Mahal); **Hulton Getty Picture Collection** pp47 (Picasso), 52 (Cotton picking), 56 (G. W. as farmer), 60 (jeans), 61 (phone calls, television); **Image Bank** pp8 (Juan Silva/Lena & Miguel), 11 (Stephen Derr/ Mary), 61 (Archive Photos/ hamburgers); **Impact Photos** pp21 (Andy Johnstone/ barman), 51 (Giles Barnard/female bank worker), 59 (Simon Shepherd/Valentines Day); **Insight** pp24–25; **Katz** p60 (Mansell/planes), 71 (Benoit Decout/ restaurants Lyon); **Sally Lack** p111 (Alice); **The Mandarin Hotel** p76; **Network Photographers** pp8 (Pierre), 20 (Peter Jordan/Scientist), 51 (Homer Sykes/man on phone); **Pictures** p72 (Chinese food); **Popperfoto** pp15 (M.C.C./family at dinner table), 55 (Bob Thomas/World Cup), 60 (Coca Cola, records, photograph), 61 (bikes); **Clem Quinn** p95 (Clem Quinn skydiving & portrait); **Quadrant Picture Library** p113; **Redferns** pp78 (David Redfern), 86; **Henry Reichhold** pp108–9; **Rex Features** pp40–1, 48–9 (Di Crollalanza/Alexandra Nechita); **The Savoy Group** p76 (Claridges); **The Stock Market** pp8 (Anna), 75, 93 (K Owaki/canyon and Mt Fuji), 93 (Great Wall, dancer), 94 (skydivers); **Telegraph Colour Library** pp11 (Benelux Press/Flora), 52 (Colorific/woman on verandah); **Topham Picturepoint** pp71 (Japanese restaurant), 79 (Beatles); **Trip Photo Library** pp7 (E James/Rafael, M Fairman/Tomoko), 8 (B North/Yasima, D Morgan/Irina, A Tovy/Lázló & Ilona), 9 (E James), 11 (M Stevenson/ Edward), 15 (Japanese family, S Grant/Mixed race family, B Seed/ Portugese family), 22, 23, 26 (S Grant/accountant), 39 (P Treanor/Pierre), 42 (D Cole/Samoan house, Mike Clement/Manola, N Menneer/Brad), 45 (H Rogers/ Tina), 51 (H Rogers/woman in T shirt), 51 (Grant/ man in office), 70 (H Rogers/S. Indian children), 71 (F Good/rice harvest, H Rogers/ship), 72 (Andrews/Gavin. H Rogers/Graham and Lucy)

Commissioned photography by:
Gareth Boden: pp6, 7 (school), 8 (Richard/Kurt), 11 (Bianca)35, 67 (school dinners), 75; **Haddon Davies**: pp37, 67 (biscuits), 89, 105; **Mark Mason**: pp10, 18, 27, 68; **Maggie Milner**: pp14, 19, 46; **Stephen Ogilvy**: p17

We would like to thank the following for their assistance:
Bell Language School, British Telecom plc, Gabucci, Leventhorpe School, Photosound